ANCIENT BERKSHIRE INNS

AND

THEIR STORIES

BY

ROGER LONG

Ancient Berkshire Inns

©1996 Roger Long

ALL RIGHTS RESERVED

ISBN 07457 5151 2

No part of this publication may be reproduced, stored in a retrieval system, rebound or transmitted in any form or by any means, electronic, mechanical, photocopying, scanning, recording or otherwise without the prior written permission of the author, nor be otherwise circulated in any form of binding or cover other than that which it is published without a similar condition being imposed on the subsequent purchaser.

Published & Distributed in the UK by:

TWM Publishing
12 Horseshoe Park
Pangbourne
Berkshire
RG8 7JW

Tel: 0118 984 4337
Fax: 0118 984 4339

Cover photograph: The Bull Inn, Standford Dingley

Also by Roger Long

1990   Murder In Old Berkshire

1991   I'll Be Hanged

1992   The Crowthorne Chronicles

1993   Haunted Inn's of the Chilterns and Thames Valley

1994   Final Commitment

FOREWORD

When one admits, nay, states with pride that one was born and bred in Berkshire, one is inclined to be the cause of disparaging remarks and sarcasm from the inhabitants of less favoured counties.

I was once asked rhetorically, from a man who should have known better. "Berkshire, isn't that the dreary and mundane county that cocoons the M4 for some fifty miles?".

The Royal County is indeed bisected by the M4, and, at its greatest breadth, hardly ten miles from the hard shoulder. But what a strip of land this is. This 'uninteresting ribbon of mundanity' probably encompasses more ancient and historical sites, more castles, roman remains and ancient hostelries than any other area of its size in the country.

From John-o-Gaunts Hungerford, in the west, through the Newbury Battle area's, Readings Abbey and Gaol, Maidenhead's notorious thicket to Windsor Castle in the east, is a journey historically enriching in the extreme. A thousand charismatic gems within spitting distance of the M4.

One criticism I've heard of the county's people is that they have a smug and self satisfied air about them. Almost one of snobbery and affluent complacency. This is partially true, but the smugness is exuded by the newcomers. Having discovered Utopia they have a right to be self-satisfied.

A well founded criticism of us locals is that we are distrustful of strangers. Can you blame us, we awoke one morning in the seventies and found that four towns (Abingdon, Faringdon, Wantage and Wallingford) had been stolen by Oxfordshire. A dozen or so villages had also shared the same fate.

A reasonably successful and talented authoress, who hadn't the good fortune to live in Berkshire, once said to me that Berkshire people are so possessive that she was surprised we didn't fence the whole bloody county off and keep everybody out.

I thought this was a damned good idea at the time, but on reflection I decided it was impractical. How could we be sure that we hadn't inadvertently fenced some aliens in. That would never do.

What makes this colourful and attractive little county the envy of its neighbours? It's churches? Partially so, architecturally they are winsome and becoming, from the exterior that is. It's prehistoric remains and ancient battlefields? Yes, to a limited degree. It's ancient towns and whimsical villages of white walls and thatched roofs? Certainly both are integral parts of its character. It's extrovert personalities? Without doubt, we have more hedonistic and lovable eccentrics per acre than anywhere else in the world. Finally its pubs? Overwhelmingly so, these are the establishments above all others that are archetypal to the county's unique and charismatic quality.

Where in Berkshire does one begin to search for these ancient hostelries? The answer is that one doesn't, one just travels a few miles in any direction and one cannot fail to come across several. The county is inundated with them, selection is the problem. Whilst researching this book I felt obliged to visit some 300 at least twice (one must ever suffer for one's art).

Having realised that there were far too many to include in one book, a stringent process of elimination became necessary. Firstly, I had the idea of discarding any building that had originated after 1800. Unfortunately I was left with a wealth of some 250 pubs. Still far too many for a single volume. I then toyed with the idea of further categorisation. Two volumes possibly, one for the east of the county and one for the west. This notion was discarded because the county had done nothing to deserve my inflicting two books on its populace simultaneously.

For this same reason, I rejected the idea of splitting the volume into two equal parts, one of town pubs and the other of village pubs. I then approached the problem from a completely different angle. Between 70 and 80 inns seemed to be an ideal number. This made selection extremely difficult indeed. On the one hand there were many charming and aesthetic old houses that were sadly lacking in any recorded legend. These frustrating and intriguing old pubs with no apparent history were reluctantly abandoned.

On the other hand, inn's with colourful histories, but with little to recommend them on the photogenic or architectural front were also sadly omitted. What is left is a mish-mash of inns that I deem to have a reasonably interesting history and are tolerably pleasing to the eye.

I hope the reader enjoys the outcome as much as I took pleasure in its extensive research.

ROGER LONG

The Hinds Head, Aldermaston

An ancient hostelry indeed and looks it. Varying alterations over the centuries have been exquisitely blended in with the existing structure. Most of today's building is reputed to date from the mid 17th century and celebrations were held at the inn at the end of the civil war.

The inn was originally named the Congreve Arms after a local family that had associations with nearby Aldermaston Court. The court was burned to the ground in 1845. The local fire fighters being summoned by the ringing of an alarm bell set in the Hinds Head's impressive clock tower. The fire alarm continued to be sounded from the inn until the brigade was disbanded in 1930.

One victim that the alarm failed to save was a drunk who burned himself to death in the local lockup which was adjacent to the inn. There was some talk of his spectre strolling the premises for a number of years, but I believe this can be put down to village superstition and vivid imaginations. The small gaol received its last guest in 1865 and has not had any functional existence since.

One of the Hinds Head's lesser claims to fame is that it was the local of John Stair, the village schoolmaster, who in 1770 produced the first William pear.

One could not leave the Hinds Head without mentioning its most famous landlord. John Wright's family had been brewing at the inn for generations. His ale was unsurpassed. Sold not only over his own bar, but in most of the hostelries in the district.

In 1912, after 40 years of personal brewing, John was disgusted when his basic products forced him to put his beer up to 2 pence a pint. John decided that this was asking too much of his customers and called it a day.

The Bell, Aldworth

This ancient village, so well described as the little village with the big heart. Aldworth was settled by the famous Flemish family, the De La Beches. A family that arrived with William the Conqueror. The De La Beches built a castle on the side of the down. The castle is gone, and so is the mighty yew that once measured 28 feet in circumference and was reputed to be some 600 years old. What remains is an old well with a depth of nearly 300 feet and the mighty carved figures that adorn the tombs in the village church.

The Bell is 14th century, a relative newcomer to the village. It is rustic and almost totally unspoilt. It's simplistic charm is undeniable and the landlord does not suffer modern proprieties. The overall atmosphere is one of parochial homespun pleasure.

The Bell is reputed to have been in the same family for two hundred years. A continuity under-valued by the massive groups of hostelries and steak houses that inflict themselves upon our most rurally attractive pubs. It is easy here to step back in time. Study the pictures of ancient village cricketers on the wall. One would not be surprised to see them wandering the street towards their favourite inn, bearded faces under schoolboy caps, discussing tactics and shortcomings.

On several occasions The Bell has been noted camera's pub of the year. It is also a favourite watering hole for knapsack walkers that descend from the ancient ridgeway to break their journey. And so it has been for centuries. May it remain so for several more.

The Hinds Head, Aldermaston   Picture by Brenda Allaway

The Bell, Aldworth   Picture by Brenda Allaway

The Bull, Arborfield

The Bull is one of the most popular inn signs in England. There is however, a misconception of its origin. It is often taken to depict and honour a famous champion beast of the locality. This unfortunately is rarely the case. Most signs denote that this was the venue in the village or town designated for the horrendously cruel sport of bull baiting. Thankfully this barbarous indulgence was outlawed in 1836.

The 17th century Bull at Arborfield stands at the junction of five roads. By far the busiest of these being the A327 from Farnborough to Reading. Settled between this maze of roads is a small triangular village green. At one stage this area constituted a pond and this is the last resting place of the Arborfield Witch.

The Witch is reputed to have been the wife of a farmer from the Swallowfield Road. She got up to all kinds of mischief. She spirited sheep and cows, turned placid dogs mad, caused milk to curdle, brought down torrents of rain to destroy crops and called up winds to blow the wigs off local gentry.

The villagers had had enough. They seized her, bound her and threw her into the local pond to drown. Having checked on the ladies demise, the villagers then placed a large slab of rock upon the corpse to stop the spirit from escaping.

Shortly after the war the village council decided it needed a village green and that the pond must go. As the water was lowered a large white stone appeared. Workmen were refused permission to remove it. Superstition was still rife in villages in the 1940's. The stone remains well beneath the earth and grass.

The Bull still enjoys an atmosphere of historic serenity despite the close proximity of the busy road. It was probably this air of imperturbability that enticed Queen Victoria and Albert to make and impromptu call, when journeying to visit the Duke of Wellington at Stratfield Saye in 1945.

The Swan, Arborfield

The older the inn the more common the sign. Years ago there was none of the modern fad of trying to think of an original if not unique name for a hostelry. Angels, Bears, Bells, Bulls, Chequers, Crowns, Falcons, Georges, Kings Heads, Lambs, New Inns (very ancient), Queen Heads, Red Lions, Royal Oaks, Swans, White Harts and White Lions made up 90% of the names in the country.

The Swan, possibly because of its regal poise, was thought to be associated with innocence and purity. In the case of the Swan at Arborfield, local geography no doubt played some small part. The village being close to the River Loddon.

Arborfield was justly proud of doing well in the Berkshires Best Kept Village competition for a number of years. The prestigious white and timbered exterior of the Swan no doubt enhanced and endorsed the villages reputation.

Just a stones throw from The Bull, this 17th century inn must have enjoyed its heyday during the coaching era. Internally it is compact with two front bars and a small stairway to a dining room at the rear. Pictures of Nelson, Wellington and other heroes adorn the bar walls, but there is no specific claim to fame with any such notable gentleman.

There is however, a tenuous possibility that some of the twisted beams were at one time part of the mighty French and Spanish fleet. There is also a rumour, probably better authenticated than the first, that George III regularly used the Swan whilst deer hunting. At this time 1780 Arborfield was still on the fringes of the ever decreasing Windsor Forest.

The Bull, Arborfield   Picture by Peter Bourne

The Swan, Arborfield   Picture by Peter Bourne

The Dewdrop, Batts Green

I once found this inn with an in-depth sense of achievement. Its secluded, almost remote position has made it a target for the adventurous amongst the pub touring public. The very atmosphere that attracts people is the same atmosphere that people destroy.

I remember The Dewdrop as having no electricity and very little else. Its log fires and oil lamps gave it an air of mystery. Its very location situated in the depth of a dark forest made it a must for a teenage schoolboy such as myself. I cycled the seventeen miles from my house to the hostelry at the age of 16, only to be told by a discerning landlord in an empty pub that I was too young to drink. This reception and a torrential downpour going home on a dark and windy night nearly circumvented by teenage ardour for such places.

The Dewdrop is approximately some 300 years old. It is built of brick and flint and is very compact inside. The spit and crackle of the log fire and its welcoming glow on a winters night is enticing indeed. It no doubt had the same effect on the foresters years ago, for whom, it is rumoured, the old inn was built.

The Dewdrop still maintains some air of mystery. Except when it is surrounded by sandwich eating tourists on a hot summers day. A back road meanders from here to Hurley, another intriguing village. There must be a dozen stories here lost in the timeless mists of the ancient woodlands. Let us hope it escapes and does not become a victim of its ever increasing popularity. God forbid there is a steakhouse chain waiting in the wings.

The Stag and Hounds, Binfield

The Stag and Hounds stands on the ancient trackway that once ran the length of old Windsor Forest. A venerable elm tree that was once regarded as the centre of the forest, stands nearby to the inn.

The oak framed building on the green is thought to have originated in the 14th century as a hunting lodge. Not being converted into an inn until 1727. The name, reminding its customers of its original function in life.

Prior to its conversion, legend insists that Good Queen Bess stopped here when returning to Windsor. She watched the local youngsters dancing around the maypole.

A second famous visitor to patronise The Stag and Hounds was William Cobbett in the 1820's. Cobbett, renowned for his 'Rural Rides', was travelling from Windsor to Reading. He described his excellent breakfast at the inn. Praise indeed from a very discerning man.

Obviously there have been changes to the exterior of the building but the interior remains much as it always was. There is period furniture, old fireplaces and heavily timbered bars. One bar top is reputed to have been constructed from coffin wood, supplied by the local undertaker. In the nearby stable room the original stalls have been upholstered and now divide the building into separate booths for diners. The low beamed ceilings and the walls play host to curios of every imaginable kind. A dozen nooks and crannies tantalisingly disappear in varying directions. All very intriguing.

The Stag and Hounds also has a very tenuous association with the case of Rosa Rose, a local lass who was thought to have wilfully murdered her baby in 1869. More of this in 'Final Commitment'.

The Dewdrop, Batts Green   Picture by Peter Bourne

The Stag and Hounds, Binfield   Picture by Peter Bourne

The Bull, Bisham

The Bull at Bisham stands a stones throw from the famous Bisham Abbey. Ancient indeed, and thought to be the home of the village mason who built the local church some 900 years ago.

A sign on the wall of The Bull opposite the car park does not claim such extreme antiquity. It states that for 650 years the hostelry has been frequented by the Knights Templar, King Henry VIII and Elizabeth I.

The notice goes on to state that royalty, nobility and commoners are all welcome, and as there is no-one commoner than I, I entered.

What a tasteful old inn this is. Ancient artifacts and modern conveniences have created a delicate rapport. A prime example is the ancient leaded lights complemented by modern double glazing.

One is greeted on entry by a large flat wooden effigy of a bull. There are pictures of short legged, terribly obese bulls everywhere. The expensive carpet shows the pattern of bull heads.

The restaurant has unique statuettes set into the walls. There are stone Chinese dragons, hares, elephants, poodles, greyhounds and even ducks. The initiator has achieved a fine balance. A few figures more would have become ostentatious and pretentious.

Also surprisingly tastefully done are the plaques set into the walls beneath the horse bass bedecked ancient beams. They bespeak uncomplicated homespun philosophy. Such simplistic wisdom, childlike and yet not profane, small brown cosy mice and other cuddly mammals are mentioned. Sickly sweet and open to ridicule in other surroundings, in The Bull they are uniquely acceptable. An example that stuck in my head could well have adorned a child's autograph album. Trite yet sincere.

> Kind hearts are the garden
> Kind thoughts are the roots

Kind words are the blossom
Kind deeds are the fruits.

The Boot, Bracknell

This attractive hostelry only just qualifies as an ancient town tavern in two respects. Firstly it is on the every outskirts of Bracknell and always seems to affirm more with the hamlet of Warfield. Secondly it is not very ancient. It has been a pub for about 150 years, but the building is obviously much older. It has been suggested that it was a foresters cottage for some 200 years previously and I should imagine, taking into account its geographical location, this was probably the case.

The sign of The Boot is unusual. There are few such boards in the country. The only other one that springs to mind is the one in Grays Road in London, frequented, as were many of the capitals inns, by Dickens. There is of course, in this neck of the woods, the possibility that this particular sign has something to do with Wellington. Not, however, according to the artist, who has singularly depicted a broken and ancient footwear on this particular board. I am inclined to put forward a personal theory based on no logical evidence whatsoever that 'Boot' may have originally been 'Boots'. This being the collective name given to servants that collected and cleaned travellers shoes (such as Sam Weller in the Pickwick Papers).

The Boot at Bracknell has a couple of eerie stories surrounding it, if not exactly connected with it. Behind the hostelry once stood Warfield Park, a massive country mansion. The building has since disappeared and a vast caravan site now covers the mansions many acres. A serving girl named Rachel was supposed to have drowned herself in the mansions lake. The lake now bears her name and is the venue for her spectral meanderings.

That of course is another story and hardly connected with the inn. The Boot however has tenuous connections with another local story. It was here that half the village gathered before they marched to Warfield Park to give the owner, Lord Ormanthwaite, a taste of 'canning'. Lady Ormanthwaite was a very popular philanthropist in the neighbourhood and it had come to the ears of the populace that the good Lord was giving his Lady a violent time. Joining another band that had congregated at the Plough and Harrow (see Reputedly Haunted Inns of the Chilterns and Thames Valley), the combined villagers headed for the park. Once there they showed their disapproval by rattling and banging buckets, washboards, shovels and any implement that made a noise, for the whole of that night.

Lord Ormanthwaite retaliated by taking the names of the ringleaders and later charging them with unlawful assembly. As to whether or not he treated his wife any better in the future we are not informed.

At the present time The Boot is a very attractive inn indeed. Extensions have been built but blend in very well with the existing building. There is tasteful wooden panelling and a parquet wooden floor. There are pictures from classical artists and two bay windows adorned with leaded lights. Unfortunately when I was last there in February 1994 both gaming machines has been broken into. Regrettably a sign of the times.

The Bull, Bisham   Picture by Peter Bourne

The Boot, Bracknell   Picture by Brenda Allaway

The Bull, Bracknell

The main footpath ridden road between Ascot Heath and Reading, meandering through moorland and forest, was responsible for coaching inns in the area, and subsequently Bracknell town itself. The Bull was such an inn.

The third of Bracknell High Street's ancient inns, its antiquated facade in stark contrast to the surrounding buildings. It is probably the last gem of the old high street. Isolated beyond belief, amongst the modern, the meaningless and the mundane. Like a friendly old character amid sycophantic plebs.

The modern, eternally watered, and revolving marble ball on its doorstep is sheer contradiction. People marvel at the sphere with their backs to The Bull before heading for MacDonalds. A terrible shame.

Internally The Bull is pleasant but not over exciting. There must be a story here somewhere but if so, I have not heard it after over 30 years of patronage. There are cartoons on the walls entitled 'Elegancies of Golf' which portray famous players at the turn of the century, mens plus fours and ladies leg of mutton blouses abound.

When a rather extensive renovation took place in 1960 an old attractive fireplace was found that was thought to be victorian. At the risk of repeating myself, the atmosphere of The Bull is agreeable rather than sensational.

The Horse and Groom, Bracknell

Now part of a chain of Steak Houses, the corporation have tried to maintain some of this old pub's charm by retaining the original beams and by hanging ancient photographs of Bracknell on the walls. There has been a limited success, efficiency and antiquity are not generally conducive bedfellows.

When researching my book 'I'll Be Hanged', I came across a reference to the Horse and Groom entirely by accident. It seems that in 1810 an unfortunate youth of 17, William Ware, was returning to Frimley from Bracknell Fare. The area then being part of Bagshot Heath and inundated with cut-purses.

The Wares party, William, his father and two others, were set upon by three Irishmen with cudgels and were beaten for some considerable time. William was knocked senseless. He was carried to the Horse and Groom where he died the following day.

It is not known whether poor William Ware is responsible for the psychic phenomena experienced at the Horse and Groom. I deem it very unlikely. I have previously related in 'Haunted Inns of the Chilterns and Thames Valley' one or two of the mysterious goings on at the inn. The culprit seems to be an elderly lady that once worked here. Her footsteps were regularly heard overhead as she went about her chores. I once questioned a lady who was regularly a babysitter there. "They were only disconcerting the first couple of times that you heard them" she replied. "After that you began to expect them. They almost seemed to be welcoming you".

There was however, a second less welcome spirit discovered by the new landlord in the late 1960's. It was a phantom tippler. A spirit with a passion for liquid spirits.

Whisky was disappearing from a locked cupboard at rather an alarming rate. When talking to the landlord some years later I suggested that when he took over he may have inherited a member of staff who had found it prudent to have had his own set of keys made. His reply was that this was unlikely firstly because he had brought his own staff with him, secondly because he had changed the locks on all cupboards and doors. Strange indeed.

The Bull, Bracknell   Picture by Peter Bourne

The Horse and Groom, Bracknell   Picture by Peter Bourne

The Old Manor, Bracknell

A notice in one of the bars informs us that this was a private residence owned by an Ascot veterinary surgeon until 1930.

The inn has recently been purchased by a restaurant chain. They are a group that seem dedicated to the retention of all that is worthwhile in the ancient properties they obtain. Such an outlook is rare indeed. Why it is that some groups think that antiquity and profit are not conducive I really don't know. The Old Manor has been purchased, altered and enhanced.

The aforementioned notice goes on to relate several other stories of the inn. One should look upon the revelations as romantic rather than factual. It tells of highwaymen's tunnels from the Old Manor to the Hinds Head, a hostelry that once stood some twenty yards away on the other side of the street.

Personally I am not a great believer in subterranean passages. The price of their construction would seem to outweigh their usefulness and financial viability. What is often mistaken for a tunnel entrance (invariably bricked up) is the access to long cool store rooms that were once a feature of ancient inns.

The Hinds Head was demolished in the early 1960's. I was one of the unfortunates that helped in the old pubs demise. Legends abounded, one that has stood the erosions of time is of a couple names Milliard, who did to death dozens of unsuspecting guests in the 1770's. Depositing their bodies in the pubs well. There is very little to substantiate this gruesome little tale except for a few bones (possibly animal) that were discovered there. From what I can remember of the demolition, the well at least existed. I cannot remember any evidence of an underground passage.

But back to the Old Manor. It did apparently feature in the religious persecutions. Several priest-holes have been discovered over the years. One is now exposed to the public and the effigy of a cassock clad figure gazes down on the imbibers below.

There have been reports, very poorly substantiated, of a low uncanny murmuring over the years. The more imaginative interpreting this as a phantom jesuit priest in prayer. It is described as a type of moaning and I should think highly justified. Imagine being stuck behind a metal grill with dozens of people swilling back beer below one.

This is not a book on the supernatural, I have already attempted that. So I shall not go on to mention the regular, who in the early 1970's was reticent to leave the bar even several months after his demise.

Please don't leave the Old Manor without wandering through the restaurant and admiring the photographs of old Bracknell. It is really worth a look.

Hinds Head, Bray

There are two schools of thought over the origin of the Hinds Head. The first substantiated by the name of the inn is that it was a hunting lodge circa 1550's. The second is that it was built as a lodging house for stonemasons as they constructed the nearby St Michaels Church. Let us settle for a compromise. It was possibly built as a hunting lodge and utilised later by the stonemasons.

The internal walls are beautifully panelled and discretely bedecked with information. In glass cases are newspaper clippings showing the Queen and Prince Philip dropping in for lunch. Another much older and smaller notice states that all shops in the village shall be closed on Wednesday afternoon for the internment of the remains of George III.

The Hinds Head also encompasses a fine staircase, a small but lavish restaurant and a baby grand piano. When I last entered the establishment on a Saturday night a guest had been coerced into exercising his doubtless talents on the instrument.

There is of course the inevitable placard referring to Brays famous vicar. This gentleman, made a household word by the song, was a notorious turncoat who under different kings changed his allegiance on some three or four occasions. First papist, then protestant, then papist again and finally protestant. He answered the charges of being a traitor by stating that it was his criteria in life to remain vicar of Bray at all costs, and, if this demanded a change of belief from time to time, then so be it.

There is some conjecture as to who this character actually was. Some think he was Francis Carswell who was vicar here from 1667 until 1709. Carswell it is said, had to adapt his views through the reigns of the last Stuarts and William of Holland. More recently, however, it has been pretty well established that the changeable vicar was one Simon Aleyn or Aleynn or even Alwyn who survived the turbulent days of Henry VIII and his three children. Aleyn had seen martyrs burned to death at Windsor and this may have helped him to remain somewhat flexible in his beliefs.

The Old Manor, Bracknell   Picture by Peter Bourne

The Hinds Head, Bray   Picture by Peter Bourne

The Pineapple, Brimpton Common

Brimpton Common is a wild and lonely place. There is an air of ancient solemnity here. It has been nurtured from the unspoken wisdom of the ancient Britons who excavated the nearby burial grounds to the taciturn shepherds that watched their flocks on the lonely Berkshire hills.

When this area was besotted by sheep in the 16th century and Jack of Newbury was keeping one hundred looms going every day to process their fleeces, shepherds were often alone for days on end. Small huts were often provided for their meagre comfort and supplies were brought out by passing carriers and drovers.

Many such huts became ale houses as the roads meandered near them to bring supplies. In all probability the Shepherds House between Reading and Sonning began life this way. As indeed did its namesake at Hawthorn Hill, the Shepherds Hut at Eton Wick and also the one at Ewelme seem conducively located.

The Pineapple at Brimpton Common is reported to have been a shepherd and drovers stopover, but there is reliable information that there was some sort of dwelling here that was recorded in the Domesday Book.

The present building does not go back to William the Conqueror but parts are very old indeed. It is a traditionalists haven. Solid elm furniture made by local craftsmen of the past. Quarried tiles on the floor, vertical and horizontal beams, ancient fireplaces and dangerously low ceilings. It really has everything.

One thing that mystifies most chroniclers is the name. I have heard several explanations, most of which are pretty inept pieces of guess work. The most plausible, but still unlikely, is that it was called after a pine forest that once covered the area. I deem this unlikely, I shall hazard a guess that the origin is based on very little provable fact.

In 1665 a Berkshire gardener named Rose grew the first pineapple in England. The Pineapple at Dorney near Maidenhead commemorates the event. Rose presented the fruit to Charles II and after a short time it became a must at the most exclusive dining tables.

Enterprising landlords that managed to gain a supply advertised it on their signs, similar in manner that the first Beaujolais is celebrated today. Perhaps the landlord at Brimpton Common was such an enterprising man. Who knows, it sounds plausible to me.

The Griffin, Caversham

Unfortunately the old Griffin was demolished in 1911 and the present one erected. This statement in no way detracts from the inn as it is today, but as can be seen by pictures in the bar, the old building was the archetypal ancient English hostelry.

The present comparatively modern building is pleasant and spacious, it's back lawns extending to the gleaming River Thames. However, it would not be included in this anthology, had the original not a story to tell as strange as any recorded.

In 1723 a stocky and jovial farmer named Jonathan Blagrave kept a farm in Upper Caversham. Jonathan was generous, hedonistic and good company. As with most popular and extrovert men, he had a couple of glaring faults in his personality, and they were to be his downfall. One was that he drank too much, the other that he was boastful and exaggerated to the extreme.

On a Saturday night in February 1723 Blagrave was returning from market. He had already inflicted his personality on several Reading ale houses before crossing the bridge and virtually falling off his plodding horse that had found it prudent to stop at the predestined venue.

Jonathan was well in his cups as he was welcomed by both landlord and regulars alike. He was well in form as he boasted of his prowess at making money in his dealings at the market some hours previously.

Unfortunately for the farmer, his rantings were overheard by three young people sitting in the inn's corridor. The trio, two young men and an attractive young woman, were down on their luck and looking for a way out of financial difficulties.

Blagrave left the Griffin about 3 a.m. on the Sunday morning. He had travelled some three hundred yards before he was set upon by footpads. His skull was cracked and his purse stolen. Badly wounded as he was, the intrepid farmer managed to drag himself to another inn, The Roebuck, before expiring.

The infant Reading Mercury stated shortly after that "three young people were took up on suspicion", and a short time afterwards that Ambrose Strange, who killed Blagrave, was to be hanged in chains at Tylers Heath. There was no mention of the other two people involved.

165 years later, in 1888, workmen digging in Woodcote Road near the murder site, excavated three skeletons, two men and a woman. The bodies had been stretched, which is consistent with being hanged in chains. There can be little doubt that these were the robust farmers assailants.

The Pineapple, Brimpton Common   Picture by Brenda Allaway

The Griffin, Caversham   Picture by Brenda Allaway

The Swan, Clewer

This pub that has an exterior that belies its ancient origin. The Swan is at least in part Elizabethan. It sits in a little pocket of affluent beauty a stones throw from Clewer Church and the river. In the church yard lie the remains of Sir Daniel Gooch, Clewers most famous son and a reported regular at The Swan.

Gooch was a railway pioneer who at the age of 20 had impressed Brunel to such a degree that he made him his personal assistant on his Great Western Railway project. Gooch was involved in the great railway works at Swindon. He became interested in telegraphic communications with America and personally sent the first cable to the new world in 1866. Gooch was also involved in the Severn Tunnel and the Great Eastern Steamship company. He died aged 73 at Clewer Park after spending 20 years as a member of parliament.

The Swan was ancient before Gooch sought refreshments there on sunny Sundays. There are reports, probably exaggerated, of tunnels, one to Windsor Castle and another to Clewer Church.

Internally the Swan seems a little uninspired, but one must seek to look around the darkened corners and absorb the inns unique atmosphere. A locals pub is this, where a man may enjoy a pint a few hundred yards and a lifetime away from the clicking cameras of the American and Japanese tourists.

Ostrich, Colnbrook

Colnbrook, this lovely old village, was saved at the 11th hour by a by-pass. There are several inns and other buildings of character, but probably the most famous, due to its infamous past, is the Ostrich.

The name Ostrich is probably the mispronunciation of the word Hospice. If it is, then it has stuck for many generations.

The Ostrich is one of the oldest inns in the country, dating back to the 11th century. However, very little of the present building dates back to that era. Having said that, most of the exterior is old, very old indeed. A walk through the yard will show you the genuine antiquity. Inside, the beams and smoke encrusted timbers place the age of the present Ostrich at about the 15th century.

It is also difficult to date Mr Jarman, the notorious host at the inn. Thomas Deloney, reputed to be Englands first novelist, mentions the landlords nefarious goings on in the late 1500's. This would seem to be some 200 years after the actual events, so let us for arguments sake place Mr Jarman at the Ostrich in the late 1300's.

Briefly, the enigmatic facts are that Jarman found a way to supplement his income by murdering selected guests. The landlord would ply the unfortunate victim with wine (in some reports he used drugs). He would then lead the man to his room and wish him good night. When the poor fellow was deep in a drunken stupor, Jarman would pull back two floor bolts, causing the bed to maintain a 45° angle, thereby depositing the victim in a vat of boiling fat below.

Thankfully, death was usually instantaneous. Having completed this part of the task, Jarman would relieve the body of valuables, deposit it in a nearby stream and then for good measure sell the victims horse to gypsies that lived on the moor.

Jarman followed his lucrative trade for a number of years before finally being caught. There are different versions as to how. One is that after a very dry period the stream used by Jarman failed to drift a body away. Incidentally, in this version the last victims name was

Coln, hence Colnbrook. A second version is that an ostlers boy heard Jarman shouting in pain after some fat had splashed on his face whilst he was about his ghoulish pursuit. Yet another version was that an intended victim was relieving himself in the corner of the room when he noticed his bed being tilted. A later and slightly more humorous reason for his capture is the suggestion that authorities approached him for no VAT returns.

Take your pick, but Jarman was caught and hanged, which seems very lenient for that period of time. He is quoted as to admitting to more than 100 murders while on the scaffold. This is probably an exaggeration, a man about to be hanged may be forgiven the odd boast or two. An educated guess at the time put the number of Jarmans victims as a mere fifteen or sixteen.

The Swan, Clewer   Picture by Brenda Allaway

The Ostrich, Colnbrook   Picture by Brenda Allaway

Bel and Dragon, Cookham

Bel (with one 'L'), as most people know, is the name of the assyrio babylonian gods Enlil and Marduk. In the story of Bel and Dragon we are told how Daniel convinced the King that Bel was an image and not a living deity. Once part of the book of Daniel the story has been relegated to the apocrypha (the septuagint or esoteric Greek version of events now much contested).

Apart from the name, the ecclesiastical associations are much in evidence. The Bel and Dragon was built (reputedly in 1417) to house masons working on the nearby church. I believe it still stands on Glebeland, land belonging to the church.

The Bel and Dragon is one of the Country's oldest licensed houses. Its original timber frame with wattle and daub walls remain resplendent from the days when the adjacent pack horse track was used by wayfarers travelling from London to Oxford.

In those days the River Thames was crossed by the nearby Lady Ferry. Sadly this no longer exists, the area where it plied its trade is now festooned by picnic sites and sailing clubs.

Cookham High street is a delight to the eye, architectural variations abound. Public houses appear every few yards. A legacy from the coaching era and the traumatic crossings of the Maidenhead thicket. The Bel and Dragon was the jewel in the crown, it adapted to the coaching era with ease.

Cookham was the home of Sir Stanley Spencer, the famous victorian artist. Spencer was born and bred in the village. His father played the organ here and reputedly enjoyed the occasional tipple at the Bel and Dragon. Today he would find the establishment little changed other than by a tasteful extension.

The bar area is three rooms, each with coal fires and old beams. The narrow frontage belying the size of the building. Real ale is available here, dispensed from imitation barrels. The Bel and Dragon is an all round atmospheric pub. It now has a large dining room with an extremely varied menu.

The Royal Stag, Datchet

Datchet is an ancient gathering of dwellings within a stones throw from Windsor. A greater percentage of its wisteria and creeper strewn cottages are still pleasantly antiquated. Shakespeare knew the village well and made it the site of jolly Jack Falstaffs ducking in Datchet Mead.

The Royal Stag is one of several aged pubs near the village green. It has several strange stories to relate, but the spectral hand at the window seems to be the best known.

It tells of a forestry labourer that dropped in for a drink on an extremely cold day. The man left his very young boy to play outside in the picturesque snow that adorned the village. Tiring of the snow and the bitter cold the child tried to attract his fathers attention by hammering on the window. The father, being now well into his cups, paid no notice. The child distraught and freezing cold, headed for a local church. His lifeless body was later found in a drift by the church wall.

On many occasions since, the boys spectral palm print has appeared on the old inns window, manifesting his final and futile plea for help.

Jeff Nichols, in his 'Mysterious Shire' related that when the imprint appeared in 1979, the glass was removed and sent to a London newspaper for perusal. The print disappeared from the original pane mysteriously, to reappear on the one that replaced it. Strange indeed.

There is also a rumour that if a photo of the print is left in the bar overnight, glasses and bottles are found smashed in the morning. Unlikely in the extreme one would imagine. Other unexplained phenomena that frequent the Royal Stag include the grave stone of William Herbert that was found at the pub and dare not be removed for untold retributions will follow. An unknown something that frequents a bedroom and bears down heavily upon the occupant and finally a toilet that flushes itself.

The Bel and Dragon, Cookham   Picture by Brenda Allaway

The Royal Stag, Datchet   Picture by Peter Bourne

Crown and Horns, East Ilsey

East Ilsey is so ancient that its origination is lost in the mists of time. Its geographical situation, high on the downs, made it a natural meeting place. Ancient roads and supposed ley lines cross and recross these bare and noble hills. That the druids were here there is no doubt. Alfred smashed the Danes here and later King James 1st granted the tiny town its charter.

In the middle ages, corn and sheep were brought and sold here, and in 1750 East Ilsey was reputed to be the largest corn market in England. It was also in 1750 that the Crown and Horns came into existence. Its unusual name probably reflecting the areas association with James 1st and the countless sheep.

The Crown and Horns was reputedly built as a coaching inn by a new turnpike. This may be so, but I am sure it was better suited as a lodging house for the thousands of farmers that travelled to East Ilsey for the sheep sales.

In 1890 an average of 400,000 sheep were sold, of which 80,000 were penned and sold in one day. East Ilsey then boasted 24 inns, sadly their number has now dwindled to three. In later years, race horses seemed more popular than sheep and the last large market was held in 1934. I believe however, there was a small revival in the 1970's.

The race horse theme continues to thrive, not least in the Crown and Horns. Internally this is an attractive hostelry. Its wooded panelling adorned with Toby Jugs, horse brasses and saddles. More recently signed pictures of actors have joined the other memorabilia, for the Crown and Horns was the setting for the BBCs racing drama 'Trainer'.

Craven Arms, Enbourne

There was once a magnificent house here owned by Lord William Craven, a man made famous for his revolutionary ideas about fire fighting. It is therefore rather ironic that his fabulous mansion was destroyed by fire in 1718. It is from the famous lord that the Craven Arms obtained its name.

It was near the village of Enbourne that the first battle of Newbury took place. The Earl of Essex, with 10,000 troops, found his way blocked by 8,000 Royalists. It was a bloody but indecisive battle and many hundreds were reputed to be buried at nearby Wash Common.

Enbourne is ancient indeed, there is even a school of thought that believes that the county got its name from archaic Barroc Wood that lay between Enbourne and Hungerford.

The Craven Arms is ancient (16th century). It is also pristine in the nicest sense of the word. It is a little difficult for strangers to find, Enbourne is a widely spread village and the Craven Arms stands on its very edge. In fact the Enbourne village sign is a few yards in one direction and the Hampstead Marshal sign a few yards in the other.

The Craven Arms was rebuilt in the 16th century, incorporating two old cottages. It is little changed since the epitome of aged romance, a microcosm of all that was colourful in old England. It is heavily timbered and seems to be a collection of nooks and crannies, slightly overbearing, almost claustrophobic on a hot day. One should then take to the large beer garden and made the acquaintance of the many varieties of rabbits on show there.

Crown and Horns, East Ilsey   Picture by Brenda Allaway

The Craven Arms, Enbourne   Picture by Brenda Allaway

Watermans Arms, Eton

Easily missed by strangers, this old inn is world famous in the Windsor district. The geographical position just north of the river and surrounded by other buildings makes it almost impossible to take a decent picture. Parking in this ancient area is of a premium.

Strangely, inside there seems plenty of room. There is quite an extensive dining area, and also several substantial alcoves, one for non-smokers if my memory serves me right.

There are suspicions of hauntings where (see Reputedly Haunted Inns of the Chilterns and Thames Valley). If so, such rumours have a more than fertile foundation, metaphysically and materially speaking. For in 1665 when the Watermans Arms had been well established for a number of years, the great plague was virtually annihilating the capital. Its fevered fingers clawed their way to the nearer provincial towns. Windsor was one of the first to suffer. The Watermans Arms being adapted as a makeshift mortuary and graveyard. Could the inexplicable rumblings, occasionally heard from the cellars over the years, be the death throws of some fevered soul in torment. I very much doubt it.

Queens Oak, Finchampstead

Magnus Maximus, the Roman Emperor of Britain, travelled the Devils Highway from London to Silchester in AD 383. He made several stops overnight and the last of these was at a clearing in the forest that was to become the village of Finchampstead. The village is steeped in history and legend. There was once a well here whose waters were thought to run red in times of imminent national disaster.

The Walters family lived here, owners of the Times Newspaper. They were great philanthropists and provided the village with the magnificent Wellingtonia Avenue that stretches from Finchampstead Ridges to Crowthorne.

The Church was rebuilt in Norman times. It sits sedately amongst the ancient oaks and yews and "where there's a church, there's a pub" people say. Finchampstead is no exception and the nearby white walled Queens Oak reflects the benign glinting of summer sunsets.

This is without doubt the only Queens Oak in the Country. Its actual age is unknown, but it does sport an ancient notice advertising early coach travel. The coach boasted that it could make the journey to London in two days, inclusive of an overnight stop in Windsor.

There is a story here of a spectral old lady who frequents the non-smoking lounge. She is reputed to have a favourite seat by the bar. A seance was held by some regulars here to try and contact the old lady. Apparently there was some success, several of the reticent and the scornful were more than a little uneasy at the end of the experiment. It is believed that the group managed to contact an old lady and her grandson who had lived nearby. Whether or not this is the old lady that frequents the lounge bar is a matter of conjecture.

Watermans Arms, Eton — Picture by Peter Bourne

Queens Oak, Finchampstead — Picture by Peter Bourne

The Pot Kiln, Frilsham

The Pot Kiln is at least 400 years old. Of these years, it spent at least 190 in the possession of the Barre family from Scotland. It gives the appearance of a private house rather than a public one. There have been the inevitable changes and additions over the years, but the overall exterior of the inn closely resembles the original.

This unpretentious watering hole vies with the Dewdrop at Batts Green for the honour of being Berkshire's most remote inn. As with the Dewdrop, the Pot Kiln has become relatively famous, purely because of its isolation. There is not another dwelling in sight. There was until the 1940's however, a nearby brick kiln, obviously where the establishment obtained its name.

The village of Frilsham is virtually an extension of nearby Yattendon. The M4 now neatly partitions them as two separate villages. There were once some interesting old chalk caves on the minor road between the two villages. Whether or not they still exist I have no idea.

Frilsham however, did find itself in the historical limelight in the 1530's. Frilsham Manor belonged to Henry Norreys. Henry was accused of having an affair with Anne Boleyn. The charge was probably false and brought about because Henry VIII needed an excuse to be rid of his Queen. Both Anne and Henry Norreys were summarily executed.

The Pot Kiln today is justifiably proud of its good name for vitals and real ale. There is an extensive and simple bar menu. Complimented by log fires and ancient photos of the inn that enhance the walls. Two separate bars remain, almost unique in this day and age. Gone forever are the days when, on entering any pub, one decided ones social status by entering either the public or saloon bar.

The Crown, Horton

Horton, a beautiful and ancient village, was made famous by its association with the poet Milton. Here three centuries ago he came as a young man drawn by the beauty of the village. Unfortunately nothing of his house remains.

The Crown is over 400 years old, which means that it was well established in Milton's time. It is frustrating in the fact that the atmosphere and age dictate that there must be a hundred stories here to be told. Once again they have been lost in the mists of time.

The Crown is a locals pub of the best tradition. There is a separate dining area, but fortunately Horton village has never really been on the circuit and its charming character is known to a precious few.

There are nooks and crannies here, and portraits abound. The light reflecting uncanny staring eyes. This is a house of charm and romantic mystery. Outside the charm continues, a wisteria covered wall gives a sense of welcoming security.

The Pot Kiln, Frilsham   Picture by Brenda Allaway

The Crown, Horton   Picture by Brenda Allaway

The Bear, Hungerford

Often when one attempts to tell the history of an ancient inn, one is frustrated indeed. The very age and appearance suggests that there must be a dozen or more stories. All lost in the mists of time, a hundred anecdotes that have not been recorded, a host of characters past unremembered beyond their brief existence.

It is therefore, pleasant to come across an inn like The Bear at Hungerford which is the very reverse of the norm. There is so much documented evidence that one wonders what to leave out. I have therefore made a sort of chronological list, hoping beyond hope that I have included the more salient facts.

In 1298 there was some type of hostelry here. It was probably called The Bear after the bear bating that went on at the time. Official records of The Bear are first tabulated in 1414. It was once owned by Henry VII, Henry VIII and five of his six wives.

In 1537 Robert Braybon, holder of The Bear at Hungerford, gave evidence of a robbery that took place between Bagshot Heath and Windsor Park. The evidence that Braybon attests is a little enigmatic and sparse. Apparently the accused pair planned their robbery at The Bear within earshot of the landlord. When they returned eight days hence, Braybon would seem to have been instrumental in their capture.

Three years later, in 1540, a goodly portion of The Bear was rebuilt. In the 1560's Good Queen Bess stayed here on several occasions (but then there weren't many places she didn't).

King Charles 1st assembled his troops here in October 1644 at the time of the second battle of Newbury. In November he left with is troops pushing Northward via Shefford to Faringdon.

In 1668 The Bear's most famous landlord William Bell made his own tokens of five different values to spend at his inn. Bell was one of the originators of this process. At one stage it was quite popular in the area.

A friend of the landlord was Samuel Pepys, the famous diarist who spent many evenings at the inn.

1685 finds landlord Bell making the news again. He sold a barrel of ale for 8 shillings to the town constable, Richard Cannon, to celebrate the defeat of Monmouth at Sedgemoor.

By the late 17th century The Bear had become a major overnight coach stop on the London to Bristol and London to Bath routes. It also became the property of the Leybourne Pophams of Littlecote. The family arms being incorporated in the pictorial sign.

William of Orange arrived by coach in 1688 to meet the Kings Commissioners. He was interviewed in his bedchamber, but the noise of the inn was not conducive to in-depth discussion. The party rode to Littlecote for dinner.

In the early 1800's, Sidney Smith the famous preacher, also well known as a journalist and wit, played a joke on The Bears pluralist owner by booking a sumptuous and vast feast. The landlord and numerous staff awaited in vain for a Dean and Archdeacon, a Canon, Prebendary, Rector, Vicar and Perpetual Curate.

In 1821 people were sleeping three to a bed at The Bear and every other hostelry in the town. The occasion was billed at the greatest fight ever. A bare knuckle contest of many rounds between Bill Neat of Bristol and Tom Hickman the gasman. Reports at the time state that 27,000 people converged on the town in a single night.

The Bear has been tastefully restored and the atmosphere remains. One could sit in a deep chair surrounded by antiques and paintings, warmed by the open fire and sheltered by the sturdy wooden beams. It would be easy to look at the vast and ancient clock and transport oneself back to many or all of the situations listed above.

The Three Swans, Hungerford

This very attractive old inn has been around for over 700 years. The one custom unique to Hungerford is it's Hocktide Court, held on the second Tuesday morning after Easter. The court elects a constable and two Tutti men. Immaculately dressed in top hat and tails, carrying poles with tutti's (west country name for a bundle of flowers) attached to the top. They are escorted by a scrambler wearing a tall hat decorated with the tail feathers of a cock pheasant. The scrambler also carries a sack of oranges.

The tutti men visit the house of every commoner, nearly a hundred of them, they extract a penny from the men and a kiss from the ladies, often step ladders are provided to approach the more coy ladies in their bedrooms. Oranges are exchanged for kisses and handfuls of coppers are thrown to the children.

A civic lunch is then held at the Three Swans presided over by the newly elected constable. A special plantaganet punch is quaffed, said to be made from a recipe dating from John o Gaunts time. Then a strange procedure known as 'shoeing the colt' is performed.

The Three Swans came into its own in the coaching era. Routes passed from North to South as well as the Bath route from East to West. An adjacent milestone shows Oxford to be 26 miles and Sarum 27 miles. A famous landlady Deborah Bear kept the old inn in 1792 and not only did well from the coaching trade but also hired out a dozen flies for those travelling to local villages.

The name, the Three Swans, comes from the 15th century when the town owned swans as well as a mass of beehives. On lammas day, the first of August, it was the constables duty to meet the men who counted and marked up the cygnets born the previous year. On the Thames this procedure is known as 'swan upping'. An interesting anecdote recorded in 1669, states that constable Thomas Oram was a little displeased when he arrived at the appointed time and found that Bulstrode Whitelock (swan marker) had forestalled him and marked the swans before he arrived.

An addition made to the pleasant exterior of this delightful old building are the bow windows that were constructed in 1960 either side of the arch. It is agreeable indeed to sit in the bar on a summer evening watching the townsfolk of Hungerford strolling the street.

The Bear, Hungerford   Picture by Brenda Allaway

The Three Swans, Hungerford   Picture by Brenda Allaway

The Black Boy, Hurley

There are four magnificent pubs in Hurley and the 16th century Black Boy is always the least mentioned. It is situated on the main A4130 (once the A423 Maidenhead to Henley Road). The facade, attractively flower adorned, is a credit to its owners. There are so very few truly wayside inns at the present time. The speeding traffic is upon them and passed before the intense driver has time to notice.

The sign unashamedly depicts a youthful negro. So many boards that used to display such signs have unfathomably decided that it is racist. Many a grinning negroid child has been replaced by an urchin chimney sweep. To me this would tend to be counter productive and verging on the hypocritical.

Paradoxically, Hurley's Black Boy is in commemoration of Charles II. Charles was very swarthy indeed and also very short and slight. He gave the impression of being a boy throughout his adult life. His mother, the French noblewoman Henrietta Maria, announced to her sister at Charles nativity, that she had given birth to a black baby. Charles had a very mixed pedigree, being a quarter Danish, French, Italian and Scottish.

It is thought that unwittingly Charles II was responsible for many of the Black Boys that festoon the country. They were known as safe houses for the Royalists. Whilst Charles was in France and Cromwell's word was law, England was not a healthy place for his supporters. Hence the safe meeting places, possibly under the innocuous sign of a happy negroid. It all sounds quite logical and Hurley is certainly ancient enough to be involved in the civil war which was chiefly staged in Berkshire.

The Olde Bell, Hurley

Anything I could say about the Olde Bell at Hurley would be deemed superfluous. It has all been stated before, many times and oft. It has adorned more books on old inns than probably any other hostelry in the Country. With, of course, the possible exception of the Trip to Jerusalem at Nottingham.

The Olde Bell is one of half a dozen claimants for the oldest inn in the Country. It is a worthy contender, having been a guest house to a local monastery that is recorded in 1135. Much of the building however, is 15th century, a mere 500 years old.

Inside, it is wooded and beamed and rooms seem to twist away in every conceivable direction. It is reputed to have a underground tunnel that departs the inn near an ancient fireplace and resurfaces at the monastery some way away. The subterranean passage has been blocked for a number of years and this has inflamed rather than thwarted the number of supernatural stories attributed to it. All sorts of whimpering nuns and howling grief stricken monks have perambulated its interior. Each bemoaning some unforgivable act he or she has perpetrated.

Nothing has actually been seen, but and American (isn't it always) who stayed here in the mid seventies reported hearing a distinct, monastic chanting. However, the witness stated that far from making him apprehensive, the chanting exuded an inexplicable feeling of peace and goodwill. So be it.

The Olde Bell is partially a victim of its own popularity. It is becoming increasingly difficult to enjoy a quiet drink at the bar of this very busy hostelry.

The Black Boy, Hurley   Picture by Brenda Allaway

The Olde Bell, Hurley   Picture by Peter Bourne

The Castle, Hurst

The Castle, one wonders at the name in this particular instance, there is no castle closer than Windsor a dozen or so miles away. It is of course, well known that Hurst (actually St Nicholas Hurst) was once part of the mighty Windsor Forest.

The Castle is 16th century. It was originally known as the Church House and was in all probability part of the ecclesiastical buildings belonging to the nearby church. A bowling green adjacent to the inn is thought to have been laid for the convenience of Charles 1st in 1628.

The Castle's involvement with the church would seem to be functional rather than perfunctory. Rumour has it that an underground tunnel once existed between the inn and the church. Not so unlikely as one may think. Bodies were laid out in the Castles 'coffin room' awaiting internment. Subterranean passages may have been constructed for convenience.

This probably gives credence to the several rumoured hauntings at the inn. A young woman is thought to have died in the coffin room and a young lad is reported to have committed suicide there. Either or both might have been held responsible for the low groans that once ascended from the vaults below.

Star and Garter, Inkpen

A traditional country inn, some 400 years old. Its popularity surged in the coaching heyday, for what is now a narrow lane running past the beer garden was once the main highway to Salisbury.

Such a pleasant and hospitable house is this to relate such an horrendous story. For in 1676 there was a barmaid here named Dorothy Newman, an attractive, if slightly promiscuous young widow. Probably scared of being alone in her September years, Dorothy set her cap at George Broomham. George was a thrifty and hard working young man who lived with his wife and son at East Woodhay, a nearby village. Broomham worked the fields near the inn and it was not unusual for him to drop in for a drink.

Here, one fateful day, George met Dorothy and the dye was cast. The comely widow enchanted and encouraged the besotted farm worker. She cast the spell that had George as putty in her hands. How idealistic it would be, she murmured, as she lay in his arms, if they could live together as man and wife.

There was however, one small problem that prevented this utopian existence. It was Martha, George's dumpy and plain but ever loving wife. Martha must go. It would be simplicity itself.

Martha brought hot pasty's to her husband each day at lunchtime. At the top of a nearby hill there was a small pool sheltered by trees. There they would wait and cudgel the unfortunate woman to death. No doubt her untimely demise would be blamed on some itinerant tramp. All would be well for the lovers.

As planned, a few days later, the couple sprang upon Martha from their concealed position in the trees. George, armed with a hickory stick, belayed his poor wife mercilessly and within seconds she was dead. The two of them then pulled the body to the pool and pushed it in. As they turned, they were surprised to see George's small son Robert standing there. He had followed his mother up the hill and now stood as if mesmerised by the horrific proceedings. This was an event that neither of the murderers had foreseen. Dorothy was the first to act. She grabbed the child and held the tiny unwitting witness under the water until he struggled no more.

Unfortunately for the couple, poor little Robert was not the only witness on the hills that day. Dorothy's two young sons had followed their mother on her unaccustomed journey. Shocked and horror stricken by the events they fled back to the village where they related their tidings to the populace.

The couple were arrested. George Broomham, a broken man since the unexpected murder of his son, told all. Dorothy Newman and George Broomham were convicted at Winchester and sentenced to hang at Coombe Hill. The Hampshire authorities had no stomach for this action, but the Berkshire people were a little less sensitive. There had long been a bone of contention as to which county Coombe belonged. If we hang the pair at Coombe, said the Berkshire authorities, then the village comes part of Berkshire. And so it was agreed.

Adjoining the Crown and garter was once Gibbet Barn. It has since been incorporated in the form of a skittle alley. It was in this barn that the bodies of Newman and Broomham were stored before burial, after spending days swinging from Coombe Gibbet as a warning.

Hardly conducive company for a convivial drink one would have thought.

The Castle, Hurst   Picture by Peter Bourne

Crown and Garter, Inkpen   Picture by Brenda Allaway

Dundas Arms, Kintbury

The village of Kintbury seems almost as old as the River Kennet itself. There are Saxon burial grounds here and the area is referred to as Holy Place in records dating back to AD 93. The Doomsday Book refers to Kintbury as Cynetanbyric and describes several dwellings and a mill.

In 1790, **Kintbury Manor** passed through descent and marriage from the Jennet Raymond family to the Dundas family. In turn the Dundas family provided England with an admiral and a member of parliament.

Charles Dundas was over fifty years in politics before retiring as Lord Amesbury. When the canal cut its way through Kintbury in 1812 Lord Amesbury was the chairman of the resourceful **Kennet and Avon Canal Company**. The inn, a popular watering hole for canal workers and bargees, became the Dundas Arms out of respect for the aforementioned pioneer.

Lord Dundas lost a little popularity in 1830 when he, accompanied by Lord Craven; Captain Houblon and a company of grenadiers, rode down on local men involved in the industrial revolution.

Men, fearful of losing their jobs, smashed machinery and set fire to hay ricks. The local yeomanry and a company of 'gentlemen' were galvanised with London troops and the uprising was put down. 100 saboteurs were surrounded at Kintbury's Blue Ball. All were arrested and later sentenced to death. After massive petitions for clemency were received only three remained under sentence at Reading Gaol. Only one, a man maned Winterbourne was finally executed (see I'll Be Hanged).

The Dundas Arms is now an extremely amicable place. It is serenely placed between the canal and the River Kenet. It is a Sunday afternoon pub where one may enjoy a pint watching the increasing canal traffic. Internally it is spacious and has a collection of old black and white photographs depicting the inn and canal over the years.

The Bear, Maidenhead

Surprising as it may seem, there are very few ancient inns in Maidenhead. The searcher for charming antiquity in this attractive town will be more than a little disappointed. The Bear however, is the one exception that proves the rule.

The hotel stands out strikingly near the end of the High Street. It's massive figure of a black bear is nearly, but not quite, ostentatious.

The Bear's history is somewhat chequered to say the least. Tom Middleton, in his book 'Royal Berkshire' informs us that, in 1489 the landlord of The Bear inn at Maidenhead was charged with asking unlawful prices. Perhaps he took advantage of a captive clientele. Travellers preferred to repair to this hostelry for the night rather than risk the dangers of the robber infested Maidenhead Thicket.

In fact highway robbery was so prevalent in the mid 18th century that in 1736 the landlord of The Bear, Thomas Darvall, was authorised to pay the sum of £20 to anyone giving information leading to the arrest of any robber within five miles of Maidenhead Thicket.

Perhaps the best known story of this ancient hostelry concerns King James 1st and a vicar of Bray. It happened at The Bear's original site of 35 High Street. The King became separated from his party whilst hunting. He wandered the forest alone before coming across the hamlet of Maidenhead and The Bear inn. He entered unrecognised and ordered dinner.

The landlord apologised and stated that he could not feed his potential customer as it was Lent. No meat was permitted and all the fish had been ordered by other guests, the vicar of Bray and his curate. The King then requested that the landlord be good enough to ask the vicar if he may be permitted to dine with him. The Vicar agreed under a certain amount of duress. However, he found his inflicted table companion both witty and congenial. Trouble came when the bill arrived and the King pointed out that he had dressed in a hurry and come away with no coinage.

The vicar was most put out, but the curate stated that he would gladly pay the strangers share in return for the good company and jocularity they had enjoyed. As he was offering his appreciation to the curate, the Kings hunting party arrived in search of him. Finally recognising his dinner companion, the vicar of Bray fell to his knees begging forgiveness.

James 1st, compassionate in all things, forgave the cleric and assured him that he would keep his position as vicar of Bray. The curate was given the vacant canonry at Windsor.

There is some speculation as to whether or not this was the famous vicar of Bray, Simon Aleyn. Aleyn found it prudent to change his religious allegiance on four occasions during the reigns of Henry VII, Edward VI, Queen Mary and Queen Elizabeth 1st. Thereby remaining in office and being the inspiration of the famous song that bears his name.

However, as it is some 60 years between the very end of King Henry VIII's reign to the coronation of James 1st, it is unlikely that this vicar of Bray was Aleyn.

A less whimsical story from The Bear tells of a fire at the inn towards the end of the coaching era. It happened in 1835 and no less that 35 horses were burned to death. One however, aptly named Miraculous, was saved and went on to work for many years after on the Bristol Mail.

The Bear today is a browsers paradise. Its bars are ancient and pristine. I can think of few more pleasurable ways of spending an hour than perusing the old inn's multitude of paintings with a large scotch in one hand and a good cigar in the other.

Before leaving The Bear, there is one final anecdote I must inflict upon the reader. A large figure of a stuffed bear disappeared from the foyer of the hotel some twenty years ago. The threadbare relic was apparently presented to some revellers from the Isle of Wight by the manager. After years in an enigmatic wilderness it finally surfaced in a museum on the island. The curator having bought it in good faith. At the time of writing, delicate negotiations are going on for The Bears return.

The Dundas Arms, Kintbury   Picture by Brenda Allaway

The Bear, Maidenhead   Picture by Brenda Allaway

Bacon Arms, Newbury

In the times when it took three days by coach from London to Bath. Towns like Newbury with its selection of inns were welcome safe havens from the fears and traumas of the road. One of the more popular hostelries was the 16th century Bacon Arms. Large and comfortable it offered a vast and varied menu to the traveller.

The Bacon Arms is commemorative of the family of that name who held the large estate of Elcot midway between Newbury and Hungerford.

Mr Anthony Bacon rented Benham Park and Donnington Castle House. He was also joint master of the famous Craven Hunt between 1813 and 1814.

The Bacons' were a finely tuned family alternating between the strange combination of warriors and inventors. Anthony was the epitome of both. For 20 years he was commander of the Donnington Castle and Newbury Troops of the 1st Berkshire Cavalry. At the same time inventing a hot water system that brought heating into conservatories. His first successful attempt being at Elcot in 1821. He died seven years later at Aberabon near Neath in 1828. The body was returned to Shaw, where it was interned in the family vault.

Following in his fathers footsteps, Sir Anthony's son Charles became colonel of the Royal Berkshire Militia.

The present host of the Bacon Arms has retained the military theme by devoting a large lounge into the Churchill Room. Portraits and memorabilia associated with the greatest old warrior of them all are displayed in abundance.

Chequers, Newbury

The Chequers' attractive Georgian facade disguises a far more ancient coaching inn. Just a stones throw from the Bacon Arms, the two old inns complemented and rivalled each other in the heady days of the mail coach. In the 1700's the Chequers boasted a carriage body shop and blacksmiths adjacent to its main building. The modern equivalent would be a garage repair shop and coach building works enclosed within an hotel complex. But to return to ancient times the Chequers for some reason found it necessary to change its name half a dozen times, amongst others, the White Horse, Lord Craven and the Elephant have at some time or other rejoiced on the board of the Chequers. At least they were all distinguishable signs of character and not the inept and unfathomable titles that today are ruining our heritage and creeping across the country like a cancer. I hear there is a move afoot to place preservation orders on some pub names. Moor power to their elbow I say.

The interior of the Chequers today behests an ambience of refined luxury. The pastel shaded lambourn dining room is the epitome of good taste and elegance. The small and well stocked bar in the lounge gives a feeling of subtle contentment. Surrounded by Forres national racing plates and sinking up to my armpits in an armchair it took three large malt whiskies before I could be enticed upon my way.

The Bacon Arms, Newbury — Picture by Brenda Allaway

The Chequers, Newbury — Picture by Brenda Allaway

Blue Boar, North Heath

The Blue Boar is a tudor inn set on one of the high points beside the Newbury to Wantage road. Internally it is splendid. It proudly boasts a large inglenook fireplace and one is surrounded by prints, paintings, horse brasses and plates. Ancient beams withhold the ceiling and there is a red brick floor beneath ones feet. Externally there have been the mandatory extensions, but they have been done with much thought and good taste. Blending in well with the original, they border the car park and are hidden from the majority of focal points.

The life size Blue Boar from which the pub got its name was one of two pillaged by Cromwells men as they passed through Yorkshire. The stone figures were specially commissioned by Lord Ingleby of Ripley Castle. On a tour of Europe his lordship had noticed the boars in Greece and had them painstakingly copied.

Cromwells men cared little for posterity or Lord Ingleby's pains and fetched the pair with them as trophies. What happened to the other figure is unknown, but the North Heath one was lodged at the inn overnight prior to the second battle of Newbury on 27 October 1644.

Cromwell himself stayed at the inn whilst the tents of his men could be seen on the downs for several miles. In the haste of the roundheads in their thirst for battle the following morning the Blue Boar got left behind at the inn, and there it has remained ever since.

There is another strange little story attached to the Blue Boar which is worthy of mention. There has long been a legend that there was a secret subterranean passageway running from the inn to a folly called 'Hop Castle' a short way away. The story was discounted as an old wives tale, until some years ago, a farmer ploughing a nearby field rolled with his tractor into an earth covered ditch.

The Oakley Court Hotel, Oakley Green

This vast hotel can only remotely be described as an inn. It is splendorous and has an almost unique setting with its lush green lawns that sweep down to the hotels personal landing stage.

I have included the Oakley Court because it has a story to tell, a most intriguing history of events that fit in with its once bizarre countenance.

Oakley Court was built in 1858 by eccentric Sir Robert Saye. He bestowed on the building mystical and ominous twisted towers. Hideous gargoyles glower down from enigmatical turrets. Saye created a mock gothic enhancement within the fringes of fear.

Inevitably there have been extensions to provide for the increasing trade but the old building remains pretty well in tact in its grotesque magnetism. It was this most horrific aspect of the building that led Bray studios to adopt it for its Hammer House of Horrors productions. Subtle floodlights and manufactured mist made the setting perfect.

Prior to this, during the war, the government took over the building and housed the French Resistance there. It was however, difficult to find staff locally as the old house had a reputation for psychic phenomena.

Oakley Court was left derelict in the mid fifties which only endorsed its outrageous looks and confirmed far more episodes of inexplicable phenomena. One local reporter writing at the time suggested that the overpowering influence of evil had caused several people to commit suicide in the nearby Thames. This is of course pure fantasy, but there were however, more deaths in the water at this spot than anywhere else on the river.

In fact a friend of mine who was then only a teenager, was summoned by a screaming woman one day. She stated that her small son was drowning in the river. My friend pulled the child out, but it was too late. He tried artificial respiration but to no avail. At the following inquest it was discovered that the unfortunate woman had already lost two young children drowned in a domestic bath.

To get on to brighter things, the Oakley Court became an hotel in the early eighties and since then has only experienced the most convivial of atmospheres.

The Blue Boar, North Heath　　　　　　　　　　Picture by Brenda Allaway

The Oakley Court Hotel, Oakley Green　　　　　　Picture by Brenda Allaway

Olde Red Lion, Oakley Green

This is one of those inns that is frustrating beyond belief for the narrator. The Olde Red Lion is so obviously steeped in history and yet little or nothing is known. Its ancient walls must have witnessed a plethora of anecdotes over the years and yet nothing will ever be related.

One can say that it is picturesque and efficient. One can enjoy a sumptuous meal in an attractive dining room that has obviously been added to the original building. One can talk yet again of ancient beams and praise the inventiveness of a landlord who has painstakingly photographed all of his regulars and pasted them on to a large photograph of his pub. But, other than stating that the Olde Red Lion was without doubt a coaching inn, there is little more to be said.

Fox and Castle, Old Windsor

A wonderful old Christmas card pub of gleaming white walls and tortuously twisted exposed timbers. Not as famous as its counterparts in the Windsor area and all the better for it.

The main part of the building was constructed by medieval masons to shelter them whilst they worked on a nearby church.

When this charismatic old building became an ale house is unknown. It was definitely one in 1780 for there is a drawing in the bar showing the inn at that time. The picture is by Paul Standby and shows a pond adjacent to the building.

The name, which is unique, is not easily explained and has no doubt been changed several times. I shall have an intrepid stab at an explanation.

The Castle part is easy, it came about by the inns close proximity to the Royal residence. The 'Fox' is a little more difficult, but here is an uneducated guess. I do not think it has anything to do with the cuddly little pointed eared quadruped. I believe that the inn is named after Charles James Fox, a late 18th century politician and reformer. It is known that Fox would do anything to further his cause, not the least of which was to make regular visits to Windsor to rub shoulders with royalty. Fox was a flamboyant and colourful personality and popular in the extreme. He must also have employed a very good P.R. man, for it is known that he once sat in the corner of a Soho pub with his wig pulled over his eyes pretending to be a tory. Here we had a man for all seasons, the politicians answer to the vicar of Bray.

Insincere or not, Fox was good for business. Multitudes followed him about. The owner of the aforementioned Soho pub, Sam House, was so impressed that he offered free beer to anyone that would vote for Fox. Nothing changes, the only time most of us meet our MP is when they are buying beer shortly before an election.

To return to Fox, some say that he retired to the pub in Soho and that the world famous intrepid Fox in Wardour Street bears his name today.

In 1992 a book of mine was published called 'Reputedly Haunted Inns of the Chilterns and Thames Valley'. I disciplined myself to the arduous task of researching psychic phenomena of some two hundred and fifty inns around the area, hard work indeed. Of the inns I visited, only fifty had anything at all worth reporting and many of these were of the most tenuous association with the supernatural. However, since compiling the book and my publisher inflicting it upon the public, many stories have come to light.

Not the least of which was a tale told to me by the bar manager at the Fox and Castle. As this is not a book of haunted pubs, I shall not go into it in detail here. Suffice it to say that it has all the ingredients of a worthwhile tale including dogs that are petrified with their hair standing on end, phantom footmen, small distressed girls appearing at bedroom doors and a tiny shoe found when an old fireplace was altered.

The Fox and Castle has it all. The charisma, the venerability, the ambience, atmosphere and a bloody good ghost story.

The Red Lion, Oakley Green Picture by Brenda Allaway

The Fox and Castle, Old Windsor Picture by Peter Bourne

The Swan, Pangbourne

There are at least four ancient hostelries in the village of Pangbourne. All however, have been thoroughly overdone by guidebooks on the County. The village is a tourists delight, but it's early antiquity is not always appreciated.

In prehistoric times, the south branch of the Ridgeway crept down into the valley at Pangbourne. The village undoubtedly came into existence because it was the only place for many miles that the Thames was fordable.

All the inns of the village are worth a visit, but in the summer they are visited far too frequently. If however, one indulges in the epicurean delights, then Pangbourne must stand alone as the village where the connoisseur is spoilt for choice.

The Swan is not the least of the above mentioned establishments. Its age is uncertain, but it's hospitality certainly is not. There can be few more pleasurable experiences than dining at its riverside bar on a perfect summers day. The conversation and chuckling children's glee, complimented by the endless rumbling overture of the nearby weir.

It was the scene that attracted Jerome K. Jerome as one of the visiting places for his intrepid if luckless heroes in 'Three Men in a Boat'. Kenneth Graham was a regular visitor and 'Wind in the Willows' was based on the nearby river. One must be void of imagination if it is impossible to visualise Mole, Ratty, Badger and the pompous Toad creeping through the long grass on some nefarious adventure.

With apologies to Edmund Spencer, "Sweet Thames, run softly, till I end my song".

The Fishermans Cottage, Reading

Some might say that to be placed beside an industrial canal within a stones-throw of the gasometer is not a particularly romantic situation for a public house. They would however, be wrong. On a balmy summer evening this stretch of the towpath is festooned by couples walking hand in hand, blissfully unaware of joggers, cyclists, dog walkers and even the aforementioned gasometer. There is a type of benign and pleasant nostalgia here, a type of tranquillity totally unexpected amongst the noisy hubbub of Reading. Blake's lock is always worth seeing and the Anglers Rest, a hundred yards or so away always supplies a worthwhile pint.

The Fishermans Cottage is some two hundred years old. It was of course, much smaller in the heyday of our canal system. It was in all probability an ale house only. It's near impossible function being to slake the thirsts of bargee's and internal navigators. Canal transport now being obsolete other than a comparatively few tourist trips, the inn now caters for the family business, the squeals of children happily piercing the air at lunchtime and early evening.

Pictures of the inn in its early salad days can be seen on the wall. It appears to be standing alone, not surrounded by the terraced houses that now cling to the canal side. The Fishermans Cottages' latent prosperity dictated an extension and in the mid 1980's a large conservatory was added to the side of the building. Purists would find this an unwelcome intrusion, but I believe that change is inevitable and should be enjoyed, particularly in this case as it has been very tastefully done.

The Swan, Pangbourne   Picture by Brenda Allaway

The Fishermans Cottage, Reading   Picture by Brenda Allaway

The George Hotel, Reading

Gone are the days when every other building in the capital of the Royal County was an ancient coaching inn. When the adventurers having braved the dangers of Maidenhead Thicket looked forward to the relative safety of one of Reading's countless inns. The town was a natural overnight stop when the early coaches plied between London, Bristol and Bath.

An ancient coach still adorns the courtyard of The George. Well preserved and in keeping with its surroundings. The old coach's turning point may still be seen. The flying machines would enter via Kings Street, the passengers would alight looking forward to a comparatively luxurious night twixt The George's famous lavender sheets. The coach would then turn into Minster Street where the horses were stabled.

Before leaving in the morning it was a common sport for the passengers to wander the few yards to the market square to goad some unfortunate in the pillory.

In 1812 William Darter, a journalist of the time, reported how Mr Moody, a coach proprietor, bought two baskets of eggs from a Mr Millard and aimed so well that the poor felon was covered head to foot in egg yolk. No doubt Mr Moody also provided such missiles for his customers at The George. As an added refinement to their entertainment he also purchased refuse from his cooks slaughterhouse.

What is not commonly known is that a day in the pillory could be tantamount to a death sentence. If a man did not have sufficient affluence to employ men to keep his face clean he stood the possibility of suffocating to death.

Unfortunately, today, The George has placed profit before prestige, heavy metal music reverberates from wall to wall. The flashing lights of the gaming machines inflame the corner of ones eye. Perhaps popularity is worth the sacrifice of peace of mind.

Perhaps it is because of the atmosphere, or possibly because of the lack of it, that The George's ghost has not been heard for several years. Ever shy and reticent to show its face, it was contented to create a feeling of cold doom and gloom in one of the upstairs bedrooms.

The Sun, Reading

Reading seems to have adopted a scorched earth policy where its ancient inns are concerned. Of literally dozens of hostelries that were truly abundant around the town in the great coaching era, less than half a dozen remain. In living memory nearly twenty taverns have gone in Broad Street and Friar Street alone. Just recently the famous and ancient 'Olde Boars Head' has joined so many of its colourful brethren. Whereas towns like Wokingham, Bracknell and Newbury have held on desperately to such tenuous links with the past and have done their best to incorporate them, albeit beside massive computerised glass towers, Reading felt no such compunctions and its characterful inns have been flushed away down silicon valley.

The Sun is a notable exception. It is an inn of character with several stories to tell. There is thought to have been an inn here since the 13th century, with an underground passage to Reading Abbey. This is quite possible as many strange doorways and archways have been discovered under the old building. There is a vast subterranean hall here that has been subsequently bricked up. It served many purposes over the decades. Most of the building dates back from the early 18th century, the heyday of coach travel. The underground hall being the stables for over 50 horses. Yet another secret passage, or even the same one, leading to an ostlers houses across the street. It is also known that French prisoners from the Napoleonic wars were kept here, but as with many inns of the time, this was just a transient place for such men.

A norman archway was discovered here in 1920 during renovation and a small cell was found in 1922. In 1948 the whole subterranean hall collapsed, fortunately for Reading's mayor, just after his visit. Bertram Mill's circus was performing in town and the elephants were stabled in the underground hall. Apparently this did not suit them, because several committed suicide by pulling at the wooden support posts and beams, causing a cave-in. A sad little story.

For an even sadder and slightly more far fetched little tale, one must go back to the 13th century and the long demolished refreshment building. Legend states that a monk from Reading Abbey fell in love with a local lady. Foregoing his vows, they used to have clandestine meetings at the inn (the monk no doubt finding the underground passage quite felicitous). However, the young girl's heart was stolen by a dashing young soldier that used to frequent the abode. The monk was heartbroken. The soldier turned out to be somewhat fickle with the ladies affections, and the damsel, in a fit of depression, flung herself in the Thames and drowned.

Ten years later the monk was passing the inn when he heard the same soldier, boasting of his many conquests. Beside himself with rage the monk grabbed him and throttled the life out of him. The soldiers final deed before expiring was to draw a knife from his belt and stab the monk grievously. A terrible wound from which the monk expired a few minutes later.

A plausible little tale with a tidy, if not happy, ending.

The George Hotel, Reading   Picture by Peter Bourne

The Sun, Reading   Picture by Peter Bourne

Turks Head, Reading

As with the Saracens Head, the sign of The Turks Head is heraldic in it origination. The emblem was emblazoned on the amoral bearings of the Crusaders. In much the same way as retired from the Eastern Wars they took hostelries. A pictorial sign of a Turk or Saracen Head would go to prove that the owner had served his country. It was also in respect of the Turk, the fearless opposition. A courtesy to the enemy that seems to have died out over the years I cannot bring to mind a "Nazi Hotel" a Fuhrer Inn or even a Goebelles or Gouring Arms anywhere in the country.

There is also a school of thought that the Inns bearing this sign were in respect to the Turkish and Algerian Pirates that brought terror to the high seas. However, personally I do not hold much credence to this rather off beat explanation!!

The Turks Head at Reading is ancient indeed, this is proven by some internal walls that were discovered to be made of wattle and daub. The inn stands on what was the main throughfare through the town but was obviously here long before the coaches rested at the establishment on their way from London to Bristol or Bath.

The Turks Head is another Tardis type Inn. The interior seeming far larger than one would assume from the outside. It is low ceilinged but widespread and its ambience makes it a must for atmosphere seeking students from the nearby university.

The Little Angel, Remenham

The Little Angel so named because of the close proximity of the other Angel. A pub a few hundred yards away across the Thames in Oxfordshire.

In the middle ages trade between villages and towns began to increase. This obviously necessitated more travelling and by the same token more overnight accommodation was needed. Traders travelled in bands, the routes between towns being dark and precarious indeed. The odds against being attacked by footpads were decreased if one travelled in company. The wayfarers worries were certainly not over when he sought sanctuary at the village inns. A nights repose was unlikely, many hostelries being owned by the most dubious of landlords. A slit throat at the most and a slit purse at the least was the order of the day.

There were of course the genuine and respectable hosts that sought to attract travellers by naming their inns after ecclesiastical signs. One would hardly expect to have ones throat cut at the Golden Cross or The Good Samaritan or even at the Mitre. Hence this made The Angel a popular sign the length and breadth of the country. Because of the reasons above one may rely on the fact that any hostelry displaying The Angel sign is extremely ancient indeed. The Little Angel at Remenham is no exception.

It is a small pub a stones throw from the river. The interior is ancient but has obviously been modified to adapt to its extreme popularity. Every corner seems to have been efficiently utilised for its never ending flow of winers and diners.

In 1752 Mary Blandy, a thirty year old spinster from Henley was accused of murdering her father. Whilst awaiting trial Mary was placed under house arrest at her home in Hart Street in Henley. On finding her door open one morning she decided upon a walk over the bridge to Remenham. She had taken but a few footsteps from her front door when she was pursued by a throng of market customers, screaming abuse and pelting her with fruit.

"Murderess, Murderess' was the cry that followed the spinster as she fled across Henley Bridge. Mary made for the Little Angel where the landlady had been a lifelong friend of her family. After frantically knocking on the door she finally gained admittance. The door was bolted against the incensed mob outside.

Mary was later rescued by the town constable Richard Fisher, but her respite was brief. Seeing her ill-decided walk as an attempt to escape, she was transported to Oxford Castle where she spent a far less hospitable time. She was lodged in a dark cell with chains upon her ankles.

Mary Blandy was convicted, sentenced and executed at Oxford in 1752. Her shade is reputed to visit three nearby sites. Her home in Hart Street, the Kenton Theatre each time there is a production of 'The Hanging Wood' (her life story), and the Little Angel where rapping on the door is thought to be those of Mary, frantically trying to avoid a howling mob.

Let me hasten to add that the rapping has not been heard for some years. In all probability the modern efficiency of the establishment has finally dissuaded Mary. This inn is always popular and crowds were never Mary Blandy's forte.

The Turks Head, Reading — Picture by Peter Bourne

The Little Angel, Remenham — Picture by Brenda Allaway

The Dukes Head, Sandhurst

Sandhurst is Berkshire's newest town, but to the families that have been there for donkeys years it is a village and will remain a village. Sandhurst is long, slim and gangling, it meanders for nearly three miles from the polar field at Wellington College to the A30 at Camberley. If one counts Cock-a-Dobby, it has ten pubs, none of which is of venerable age. The oldest, although it doesn't look it, is the Rose and Crown. The building has been so modernised on so many occasions, there is little or nothing of the original structure remaining.

The Dukes Head, nearly opposite the Rose and Crown, is of indeterminate age, but it has stables that run for some fifty yards behind the pub and it has been included because of the story it has to tell and because of its personal associations with yours truly.

My maternal grandfather lived a stones throw away in New Road that runs adjacent to the Dukes Head. He had the first car and vehicle repair shop in Sandhurst. Unfortunately, for business purposes, Granddad's workshop was next to the Rose and Crown and opposite the Dukes Head. A pleasant geographical situation for a social life, but in Granddad's case, one hardly conducive for business efficiency.

My Grandparents were great friends with Mrs Blake, the landlady of the Dukes Head. There was always something strange about an upstairs bedroom. One of Mrs Blakes three daughters, incidentally, a retarded young lady, used to describe apparitions she saw on the ceiling. There is a long and intricate story about Mrs Blake, Mrs King (her friend) and my grandmother. It involves Charlie Peace, the double murderer, some stolen cameos and a story of romantic legend, but as I have dealt with it at some length in 'Haunted Pubs of the Chilterns and Thames Valley' I shall not inflict it upon the reader again.

However, a little story that is worth repeating occurred in 1970. The landlord had friends staying with him from up north. Whilst drinking in the lounge bar they noticed in the mirror at the back of the serving area a customer, wearing a trilby, in the public bar. Thinking to go and converse with 'a local' they walked through the hall to the other bar. The little man was gone, although there was no way he could have left the premises without meeting them. This same phenomena subsequently occurred on two other occasions. The visitors approached the landlord and various other patrons with their story. After submitting a full description, the agreement was unanimous, the mysterious imbiber was a regular who had died some years previously.

Rackstraws, Sandhurst

This complex has changed its name many times over the last decade, but I will stick to the name Rackstraws. By way of an aid to a geographical location I believe at the moment the property basks in the name of Treetops. It is an eating house, bar and nightclub. A far removed usage indeed from the original ancient Rackstraw Farm.

As Rackstraw Farm, the owners had eked out a mediocre living for over 150 years. The metamorphosis took place in the 1960's. This of course does not make it an ancient inn by any yardstick whatsoever, so as with several others it has been included for its unusual little story.

Soon after the inn's opening a photograph was taken of the ancient ovens that remained there. It was a publicity exercise for an advertisement in a trade paper. When the picture was developed a clearly defined skull was seen in the oven recess. In this particular case I am sure there was no jiggery pokery involved. Admitting only that nowadays virtually anything could be done with a photograph, 20 odd years ago it was not quite as simple.

I should like to tell the reader of some horrific murder in the vicinity, or of some local person or even traveller going missing in the area. Unfortunately I cannot. As far as any records show, Rackstraws was a serene and sedate old farmhouse that turned into a rather noisy leisure complex. Nothing more.

The Dukes Head, Sandhurst   Picture by Peter Bourne

Rackstraws, Sandhurst   Picture by Peter Bourne

The Pheasant, Shefford Woodlands

A beautiful hamlet situated, as its name suggests, in woodlands above the Lambourn Valley. At the beginning of the century a mere 70 people lived in the village and there are not many more today. The vicinity could once be fairly described as remote, but the coming of the M4 and its nearby junction has brought a limited popularity to the village and its picturesque Pheasant Inn. Thatched and made chiefly of wood the inn was once known jokingly as the boarded house.

It was in the nearby woods that the dastardly Wild William Darrel came to grief whilst out hunting. Darrel kept Littlecote House, and although he came from a long line of gentry, he was a famous ne'er do well, a gambler and deflowerer of winsome maids. He was however, a man of strength with a vicious temper and the inbred ability to do evil.

The story goes that he caused his men one night to abduct an old midwife from Shefford Woodlands and carry her blindfolded to Littlecote. Once there she was taken to a room where a masked lady lay in the last throes of childbirth. The old lady (Mrs Barnes) set about her business and shortly afterwards an apparently healthy child was born. To her astonishment the man demanded that she place the child on the open fire. She twice refused, then the man, in a fit of temper, tore the child from her arms and thrust it into the furnace. A few minutes later the mother also expired.

A shocked Mrs Barnes was escorted back to her cottage, but not before she had surreptitiously taken a small cutting from one of the curtains. Strangely enough the old lady said nothing about this experience until she was on her death bed some 12 years later. Had she one wonders retraced her footsteps to Littlecote House and been blackmailing Wild Will ever since. If so, it was a dangerous game, she knew he was capable of murder. There has been much speculation as to the name of the lady, but nothing conclusive has emerged.

Darrel was never convicted of the murder of the child, but he quickly went down hill afterwards. He lost Littlecote and spent some time in a debtors prison. He died when his horse threw him when taking a style at Shefford Woodlands. Rumour dictates that the horse shied at the apparition of a burning baby.

The Black Boy, Shinfield

Another pub where the exterior belies its ancient pedigree. The Black Boy stands on the Farnborough Road from Reading, this was once a coaching route of minor importance, but of sufficient popularity for there to have once been a smithy opposite the old inn. Smithy's were of integral importance when coaches were horse drawn.

The present landlord is justly proud of his pub and has shown sufficient interest to study the history of the house. A pamphlet has been produced and it is from this source that I have unashamedly gleaned some of the following facts.

A leaflet or pamphlet is a good idea and it is a pity that other hostelries have not adopted it. In this particular one we are informed that in 1769 the Black Boy was leased by William Simonds of Reading for a princely sum of £5 10/- a year.

In my teenage years Simonds were a fine and prolific brewery. Their boards with the famous hop leaf trade mark adorned pubs in some seven or eight counties. Later, they were bought out by Courage and Barclays, who had also swallowed up the small Nicholsons Brewery of Maidenhead. The Black Boy was sold by Courage to its present owners Moorlands in 1991.

The inn was definitely around in the times of Charles II, and it is from this short and swarthy gentleman that many such boards took their names (see the Black Boy at Hurley).

However, Shinfield's Black Boy is unique when one considers its sign above the door. It is the carved wooden figure, purported to be a negro complete with short skirt, neck chain, feathered head and besporting a long stemmed church warden type pipe.

There is a replica sign, less weather beaten, in the bar. In the 18th and early 19th centuries it was the mode to bring African slaves to England and use them as valets and footmen in the bigger houses. Pubs also used them as boot boys and grooms. It has been suggested that the figure at the Black Boy is the effigy of some revered and greatly appreciated servant. I deem this most unlikely. Nobody carves effigies of their servants.

I personally agree with one of the suggestions in the pamphlet which is that this is a Red Indian tobacco advertisement. I do not think that the features are particularly negroid and the attire is much more in the tradition of Sitting Bull or Crazy Horse. In-fact I have seen the spitting image of this figure outside an antique shop near Toronto. Indian signs once adorned every tobacco shop in the United States and many crossed the pond as Victorian souvenirs. The Sioux and Cheyenne were addicted to tobacco (hence the peace pipe and war pipe amongst others). In-fact Red Indians that gave up the weed often carried tobacco with them to emphasise their strength of character. What could be more appropriate for a cigar merchant than a wooden indian. In the case of the Black Boy at Shinfield I believe it to be a souvenir that has been adapted in colour from its mahogany to black. Having said this, I have also been told by a curio dealer in Lambeth that some cigar store indians were originally painted black.

The Black Boy today has a large front bar and a sizeable restaurant at the back. The latter I believe is an extension of the original building. Both rooms are comfortable and practical, if not luxurious. It must have been a very spartan establishment indeed in 1833 when Ismabard Kingdom Brunel met his surveyor here whilst constructing the Great Western Railway. I wonder what the old genius would make of the M4 rushing by only yards from the carpark. We shall never know. Vast changes have taken place since the inns wisteria tree was planted in the rear garden. It is reputed to be one of the oldest in the country.

The Pheasant, Shefford Woodlands   Picture by Brenda Allaway

The Black Boy, Shinfield   Picture by Brenda Allaway

The Bull, Sonning

Sonning is ancient and picturesque, but for my taste it is little too much in the old chocolate box style. As with many villages, it has a reputed association with Dick Turpin. Legend states that Dick's aunt lived here at The Dog inn. When he was hotly pursued one evening, Dick dropped his horse off at his aunt's underground stable and somehow crossed the river on foot. Personally I find this story a little difficult to believe. Turpin was a low life villain and cut-throat who committed the majority of his atrocities in Essex and Hertfordshire, very rarely adventuring west of the capital. He was a poor horseman and his romantic ride from London to York is pure fiction.

The Dog Inn was factual enough as it is mentioned in several old surveys of the village. Unfortunately it has disappeared with many of its greatly mourned companions.

The White Hart, alongside the river, is mentioned in an old deed as long ago as 1100. Apparently it was the home of 'Elias the Ferryman' who plied his trade long before the bridges were built. The White Hart is now the Great House Hotel.

The Bull is probably late 14th or early 15th century. It is adjacent to and owned by the church. In fact the churchyard was originally part of the Bull's courtyard.

It is said the hostelry was built for the lodging of Pilgrims who were about to be blessed by 'St Sarlic'. St Sarlic in its turn being a corruption of 'Sigeric', the then time Saxon Bishop of Sonning.

The Bull was the venue for ecclesiastical celebrations when the Bishop of Salisbury called in later years. Apparently this was quite a frequent event. A sumptuous meal was prepared and the wine flowed freely for several days. Even in those days there was class distinction. It is well documented that the squire and local dignitaries dined upstairs, whilst the villagers made do below.

The Bull today is little changed. The rambling white walls and outer timbers remain. The interior is somewhat small, there are massive beams and open fires, and paintings by local artists adorn the walls.

The Bull is a Christmas and summer evening pub. Indeed an inn for all seasons.

The Old Boot, Standford Dingley

This is a truly beautiful old inn situated within rural Berkshire at its best. Over its 250 year history, the Old Boot has had several extensions and now houses an attractive restaurant with the most comprehensive of menus.

Possibly in former years the Old Boot projected a less than pleasing aspect. For many years the old inn was reputed to be haunted by a local man who hanged himself in the pubs orchard, but to put at rest the would-be patrons that are about to experience a gastronomic indulgence and find such episodes unconducive. Let me hasten to point out that no ghoulish phenomena has been experienced for many years.

The Bull, Sonning   Picture by Brenda Allaway

The Old Boot, Standford Dingley   Picture by Brenda Allaway

The Bull, Standford Dingley

Another frustrating pub. I am sure there must be a story or two here. The atmosphere is ancient and charged with the indefinable magic of yesteryear.

The Bull is very old, reputed to be 15th century. There are some original timbers here and even a wattle and daub wall. This is a rarity indeed, as most of the pubs of that era have usually been much altered inside, even if their exteriors are original.

Another rarity of The Bull, is the game of 'Ring the Bull'. This is an ancient game once played regularly amongst farm workers and the like. A ring taken from a bulls snout is suspended from the ceiling by a piece of cord. A hook is placed on a wall and competitors attempt to swing the ring over the hook. The rules are pretty basic and its one of these things that looks simple until one tries.

'Ringing the Bull' was played until recently at the Crown and Anchor at Dell Quay in Sussex. It now seems to have drifted into obscurity along with so many simplistic but thoroughly enjoyable pub games.

The sign of this inn would seem to be unique. Unless I am mistaken the nearly indiscernible board depicts a bulls head on one side and an equally charming bovine backside on the reverse.

The Bull, Streatley

Streatley is a beautiful village surrounded by hills. From here one can look down upon the silver Thames gliding towards the gorge at Goring Gap. A sight shared by Britons, Saxons, Romans and Danes.

There was once an ancient nunnery here which has unfortunately disappeared, giving way to a group of walnut trees. It was from this nunnery that an errant nun made her way to the Bull Inn to meet with a novice monk until they were caught and slain, probably in a most tortuous fashion. They were laid to rest in the grounds of the inn where they had enjoyed their clandestine meetings. Two yew trees were planted upon the graves and they can still be seen in the garden of The Bull. There is a legend that on the anniversary of their demise, two spectral figures are seen to arise from the earth and walk hand in hand into the haze.

The picturesque old Bull stands on the A417 from Reading to Wantage and it was down this route in 1833 that a young farm labourer George King was being transported. King was accused of the horrendous murder of a Wantage landlady. Ann Pullin, owner of the White Hart, had been decapitated by a beanhook for the few shillings she had about her person. All evidence pointed to George King her lodger. He was arrested and transported to Reading by cart. It was a long and thirsty journey, so a stop was made at the Bull.

King, handcuffed between two officers, noticed a picture on the wall that resembled greatly his victim. He went crazy, screaming at the picture, saying that she had come back to haunt him and that he would kill her again. King was restrained by the officers who later proceeded to Reading where he was tried, convicted and hanged for the crime.

Let us finish on a lighter note. The Bull is also fondly remembered in several stories about the Thames. It was reputed to be a favourite of Kenneth Graham of Wind in the Willows fame. It is also mentioned in Jerome K. Jerome's three men in a boat, where Montmerenly states that he has eaten here much to his satisfaction.

Little has changed in the architecture of The Bull. The old pump in front of the building is still capable of drawing water from a great depth. Travellers still pass by, greater in number and at higher speed than the old coaching days, but, as affirmed by Montmerenly, one can still wine and dine very well here.

The Bull, Standford Dingley Picture by Brenda Allaway

The Bull, Streatley Picture by Brenda Allaway

George and Dragon, Swallowfield

The George and Dragon stands on the outskirts of Swallowfield village. The village where Mary Mitford, the descriptive novelist, dramatist and poet, spent the last four years of her life.

The George and Dragon has a somewhat personal association with yours truly, albeit a rather tenuous one. In 1919 when my mother was an agreeable seven year old, it was a common practice for her father Harold Timms to take the whole family for a Sunday lunchtime drink. My grandfather was one of the original motor traders and it was his habit to offer to buy various cars. Very often from publicans as this was the profession with which he spent a good deal of his time. Such a deal had been struck with the landlord of the George and Dragon. When my grandfather arrived with his family to collect the vehicle an astounding sight met his eyes. The landlord was fleeing from the house followed by various items of crockery. The aggressor, the landlady, appeared with a terrible gash across her throat. Obviously the victim of the landlords attempt at murder. The police and an ambulance were called and the landlady departed for the Royal Berkshire Hospital while her husband departed to Reading Police Station.

When researching my book 'I'll be Hanged' I came across this case in a copy of the Mercury. It seems to have had a comparatively happy ending. The landlady survived the assault and the landlord spent a comparatively short time deprived of his freedom. Whether my grandfather ever complete the deal with the car or not I do not know, but inevitably the George and Dragon received the nickname 'Cut Throat Kates', a pseudonym that has lasted to this day amongst the locals.

I visited the George and Dragon one Sunday lunchtime in October and nothing untoward happened I am pleased to say. Nothing that is, unless you count the unexpected appearance of a very jovial local vicar followed by his small and rather aged flock. After ordering a pint he led his disciples into a back room where they settled down to a very large and delicious smelling lunch.

I returned to study some of the memorabilia on the walls which was general rather than local I am afraid. There is one rather striking photograph of Sir Arthur Russel (obviously one of the Russel's of Swallowfield Court) driving the villages first car circa 1902.

George and Dragon signs are numerous and popularise the days of chivalry in England. Saint George of course being our patron saint. His day being 23 April when every Englishman swells with pride and nationalism. And, of course, totally ignores the fact that our George was born in Italy and is also the patron saint of Aragon and Portugal.

The Old Chequers, Thatcham

The large village of Thatcham is ancient indeed. The Thatcham Hundred, one of 22 in the county, is mentioned in the Domesday survey. We are informed that the area possessed 16 manors, 5 churches and 14 mills.

Unfortunately the village was decimated by the black death in the 14th century. After which Thatcham never seemed to regain its appropriate status in the county. It's geographical position however, between Newbury and Reading on the Bath Road, made it's inns popular with coach passengers during the 17th and 18th century.

One such inn is the Old Chequers situated at the western end of the main street. This is archetypical of the British inn. I wish I knew a story of the building, but this failing I shall attempt to describe an indescribable atmosphere.

The inn gives a feeling of venerable great age. The beams with the supports seem to have been grotesquely twisted into their functional positions. Aged floorboards support a dozen variously shaped seats mostly either box or bench like. Dark passages mysteriously depart in all directions and the half light inspires the enigmatical lure of the romantics.

There are a dozen places one could sit and not be discovered, watched only by the stern eyes of the faded celebrities on the wall. I personally straddled a bench beneath the disconcerting but watchful eye of John T. Sullivan, the ancient pugilist.

Is there always a tiny crack in perfection? Is there always one short-coming in paradise? Yes indeed. In this case it is the noise of the electric gaming machines. One wonders if financially they really are a necessary evil.

The George and Dragon, Swallowfield — Picture by Brenda Allaway

The Old Chequers, Thatcham — Picture by Brenda Allaway

The Swan, Three Mile Cross

Three Mile Cross probably attained it name by being on a crossroad approximately three miles from Reading. It strides the Basingstoke Road, but the little settlement has now, thankfully, been bypassed and left to try and regain its individual character. A character that Miss Mitford loved and described so well in Our Village. Miss Mitford lived with her spendthrift father in a cottage adjoining the Swan Inn.

The inn is once again white and timbered and once again gleaning its name from the nearby River Loddon. An unusual aspect of The Swan is its capacious car park, a most unusual convenience among ancient inns.

There are two bars with several alcoves leading off, all worthy of inspection. One has cartoons depicting 'Mr Tom Noddy's first day with the hunt' which shows the predicaments likely to be encountered by a not too bright novice huntsman.

Nearby is the open fireplace, and what I should judge to be the original inn sign. There is an ambience of tranquillity a few hundred years and a few hundred yards away from the bustling M4 to the north.

The Greyhound, Tidmarsh

The tiny hamlet of Tidmarsh has existed since Norman times and the Greyhound has been around since the 12th century. It was then a church house called The Grid Iron, the emblem of St Lawrence. It withstood the black death in 1240 and witnessed for years the pleasant summers when monks from Reading Abbey made wine from the village vineyard.

The Greyhound became an inn in 1625. It has changed little since then. It is a brick construction, timber framed, the thatch on the highly angled roof sweeps almost to the ground at the rear of the building.

The interior is timbered with exposed beams. Low doorways make one aware of the old adage 'duck or grouse'. A plethora of different attractive passages and small rooms seem to disappear in intriguing profusion. The Greyhound is a mecca for atmosphere seekers.

The Swan, Three Mile Cross   Picture by Brenda Allaway

The Greyhound, Tidmarsh   Picture by Brenda Allaway

The Bell, Waltham St Lawrence

The Bell is a 14th century, overhanging, timbered inn. A contender for the oldest inn in the country. It is the archetypical village pub. In fact it was bequeathed to the village of Waltham St Lawrence in 1633. Ralph Newberry, master printer to Elizabeth I and James I imparted it as a gift.

Parking is difficult here. The Bell forming part of the small village centre with some ancient cottages, the village church and what used to be the local stray animal pound.

In the churchyard lay the remains of another local benefactor and regular caller at The Bell. John Newberry (no relation to Ralph Newberry) was the counties first children's publisher. It is probable that 'Goody Two Shoes' was his creation. Newbury rejoiced in the friendship of Oliver Goldsmith and Dr Johnson, both of whom visited him at Waltham St Lawrence and in all probability supped with him at The Bell.

One is a little disturbed by the close proximity of what was the local animal pound. Roaming domestic animals were tethered here whilst waiting for their owners to retrieve them. One can imagine the din ensuing as one tried to quaff ones pint.

Inside The Bell one is greeted with an atmosphere of pristine antiquity. The panelling covering most of the walls has an air of timelessness. It is possibly ecclesiastical. I am no expert, but it is pleasing to the eye, as the open fires in each bar are pleasing to the body, and as the vast selection of various scotch whiskey's are pleasing to the inner man.

The Yorkshire Rose, Warfield

Warfield is an ancient village. Large, well spread (once taking in Bracknell High Street), but thinly populated. Even more sparsely populated after 1339 when the black death put paid to half the villagers.

In recent years Bracknell has spread ever more hungrily along the villages borders, consuming the aged and revered, replacing with the modern and mundane. There are however, several attractive old buildings left. The beautiful old regency building Warfield Hall springs to mind, sedate in its uniformity.

The Yorkshire Rose once again on the side of the ancient Forest Road, is a mere teenager as a licensed premises, but aged indeed as a historical building. The Yorkshire Rose survived as a tea room prior to the early 1980's when the owner put it up for sale and a licence was applied for and granted.

The building itself is some 250 years old, but a previous construction went back to the middle ages. It is thought to have been a staging post for travellers that journeyed the wild trackways of Windsor Forest. Monks are reputed to have supplied sustenance here. A supposition born out by the many monastic place names in the district. Priory Lane is a few hundred yards away.

There have been the inevitable hauntings over the years. A cowled figure dressed in black has been sighted and the occasional inaudible chanting has been heard. Even a little poltergeist activity has been experienced.

All seems to have settled down now. The Yorkshire Rose is well worth a visit for a reasonable meal or just a quiet drink.

The Bell, Waltham St Lawrence   Picture by Peter Bourne

The Yorkshire Rose, Warfield   Picture by Brenda Allaway

The Bull, Wargrave

I have often heard the criticism of Wargrave that so much of it is privately owned, that it is impossible to reach the river. I deem this censor justified to a degree. It is difficult, not impossible to approach the Thames. Gone are the days of Jerome K. Jerome when elegantly dressed women and blazer attired men festooned the banks with sartorial grace.

One of several coaching inns is The Bull. It is situated a few hundred yards from the White Hart on the opposite side of the street.

Timber framed with a window overhanging the corner footpath. The Bull is well described as compact. The inn has been dated as 15th century, but once again extensions have manifested over the years.

Internally it is exquisite if slightly lacking in space. Some unusual bovine cartoons bedeck the bar room walls. It also has, or rather had, some paranormal activity. The story is a rich one that relates how the landlady in the 1820's indulged in an illicit love affair until discovered by the landlord. Whether the pair were caught in flagrante delicto or whether the evidence was merely highly circumstantial we are not informed. However, the landlord showed his wife the door, forbidding her ever to return to the inn or their young child. She died of a broken heart, but for some time her spirit returned to weep and wail in an upstairs bedroom. Nothing lately I have been told. Its a good story anyway.

The White Hart, Wargrave

Wargrave, this beautiful and traffic frustrating village borders the Thames, which has no doubt added to its popularity over the years. It was popular indeed with Madame Tussaud, daughter-in-law of the lady of the waxworks fame. She is buried in the churchyard.

The village was also popular with the rakish Earl of Barrymoore. A man with a mischievous sense of humour and apparently limitless finances. He was reputedly fond of firing his pistols at the village inn signs. It was the Earl that brought an elaborate and expensive theatre to Wargrave at a cost of £60,000, an unbelievable amount of money in 1782. The theatre boasted George IV as its patron. He regularly made the trip by coach from Windsor.

There are many coaching inns around the area, not the least of which is the White Hart in the centre of the village. It is ancient and pleasing to the eye. Its external architecture obviously spanning several centuries. Slightly out of place, but still relatively ancient is the defunct and hand operated petrol pump at the front of the building.

The sign depicts a white hart wearing a gold collar. The story goes that a particular white hart gave the king an exciting and perilous chase through the forestry surrounding the inn. When the animal was finally cornered the monarch refused to let it be slain. He placed a gold collar around the animals neck so that it would be instantly recognised and not hunted again by royal decree. I would have thought that putting gold around an animals neck and letting it run wild would ensure its demise within minutes, but its a nice story.

On entering the White Hart one is greeted by the bar and reception area. To the right is the open fired Cavalier restaurant. A Franz Hals inscrutable masterpiece gazes expressively down on the diners. To the left of the entrance, in the bar area, characters of Dickens created personages observe the imbibers from the walls, and for some enigmatic reason an ancient copy of the Times announces the 'British Victory at Waterloo'. It all fits in rather nicely and is a compliment to somebody's exquisite taste.

The Bull, Wargrave   Picture by Brenda Allaway

The White Hart, Wargrave   Picture by Brenda Allaway

Five Bells, Wickham

The beautiful old hamlet of Wickham nestles astride an ancient roman highway. Its main claim to fame lies with its somewhat eccentric vicar the Reverend W. Nicholson. In 1862 this whimsical minister bedecked the north aisle of St Swithuns church with eight papier-mache elephants. He looked upon them as angels and claimed they represented such human qualities as fortitude, docility and strength.

The Five Bells is a fairly uncommon name for a pub, whereas six, seven and eight bells abound throughout the country. The only specific story I can fish up, is a nautical one. Apparently at 6.30 in the dog watch (2 short watches between 4 pm and 8 pm) five bells was a signal adopted by mutineers in 1797. The officers forestalled this by insisting only one bell was rung. Why this should have a bearing on the name of a pub so far in-land I really do not know.

In the case of the Five Bells at Wickham, I will offer a more mundane explanation. It is possible that at one time the bells of five different parish churches could be heard from the spot.

The Five Bells is mostly 18th century, but parts of it are much older. It gives me the impression that it was once three terraced cottages that were probably taken over one by one as the hostelry extended. I have no evidence for this, but it was not an unusual event, especially in the 18th century.

Today the building is thatched and low beamed, with a large and enticing fireplace. The menu is extensive and fresh lobsters are a speciality.

Adam and Eve, Windsor

This small inn directly opposite the castle walls seems as old as time itself. It is in fact 15th century, but there must have been numerous modifications since then.

The situation of the Adam and Eve in close proximity to the Theatre Royal has made it a popular venue for thespians over the years. Signed photographs adorn the walls. I personally enjoyed a pint with George Cole looking over my shoulder.

"This is an ancient inn. Has it any ghosts?" I enquired of the landlady. Throwing caution to the wind and years of experience that have dictated never to take the direct approach.

"Certainly Sir" she replied, "But we seem to get along without disturbing each other too much".

I assumed she meant the living and the dead in this establishment had created a type of harmonious rapport. It is not unusual and I pursued no further.

For a building of 500 years or more, there would seem to have been very little reported activity over the years. The sign of Adam and Eve became an emblem of The Fruiterers Co many years ago. Fruiters being the forerunner of our modern day greengrocers. I speculate with no more evidence than above that the Adam and Eve may once have belonged to a fruit seller who later obtained a licence.

There is one piece of history attached to the Adam and Eve. It is stated on a placard typewritten script on the wall. It is near a signed photograph of Jimmy Edwards complete with cane and moustache. It states that on 1 March 1817 the premises were burglarised. Entry was made via the rear wall and a large amount of liquor and rum was removed. Later a man with an evil record named Lambeth was being held in custody in connection with the said offence.

We shall never know if the evil Mr Lambeth was convicted and what punishment may have been inflicted upon him.

On reflection of the many Adam and Eve signs throughout the country, one often wonders why Adam is depicted with a navel. Eve also for that matter.

The Five Bells, Wickham   Picture by Brenda Allaway

The Adam and Eve, Windsor   Picture by Peter Bourne

Three Tuns, Windsor

The Three Tuns is reputed to be the oldest building connected to Government in Windsor. This attractive old inn, not a stones throw from the castle, has been around since the early 1500's. It has been in turn, the town hall, the guildhall and once it was the mayors abode.

In the 17th century it became an inn. One inn in a town of countless ancient inns, but an hostelry with a history. During excavations in the yard, a disused timbered well was discovered. A timber from the structure bore the following inscription. "This well fell in 1799, but the source of good cheer goes on forever".

The good cheer was still surviving well in 1994 when I last visited it.

Two Brewers, Windsor

This is a beautifully situated little pub, close to the castle and the royal mews, in congested little Park Street (an ironic name for a place where you are likely to get wheel clamped). The Two Brewers is also in close proximity to the start of the Long Walk, a never ending (3 miles) carriage drive from the castle to the Copper Horse (a statue, not a pub). The Two Brewers is a welcome respite for anybody fool-hardy enough to attempt the feat on a hot summers day.

Naturally the history of Windsor has filled volumes and the Two Brewers has witnessed the vast majority of this. It is therefore frustrating that so little of the pubs past can be traced. We know that the hostelry is 17th century and there is a record on the wall of a lawsuit in 1887. It tells in some detail of the then time landlord Henry Carpenter, who was apparently libelled by a man named Holmes, the Queens librarian. Nothing else seems to be known of the old inns history, how disappointing.

Three Tuns, WindsorPicture by Brenda Allaway

Two Brewers, WindsorPicture by Brenda Allaway

Sir Christopher Wrens House Hotel, Windsor

Probably the most romantic hotel on the River Thames. Being incurably afflicted by romance myself, I nip in for a drink or the occasional meal, finances permitting. There is a plus ambience here that embraces one upon entry.

The Orangery restaurant that overlooks the river in an unsurpassable venue for young lovers. The cocktail far and adjoining lounge gives one the feeling of unashamed opulence. It is a comforting feeling on a summers evening strolling the public rooms and appreciating the pictures of Wrens achievements on the walls.

This benign atmosphere of style and comfort belies the rather chequered history of the hotel. For many years the building was thought to be cursed. Once a private house, it was owned by a family called Cheshire. Members of this unfortunate family were suddenly stuck down by mysterious illnesses and tropical diseases from countries in which they had never travelled. One of the daughters gave birth to an illegitimate child, this event was followed by a mental breakdown. The child died in infancy and its mother failed to recover. She was kept under a sort of house arrest and only let out in the garden in the very late or early hours. Mr Cheshire nearly died of food poisoning, whether administered by accident or design we shall never know. The unfortunate man found his finances rapidly decreasing and moved to a smaller property. Another of his daughters, engaged to a peer, was jilted at the last moment.

The curse however, was apparently attached to the house and not the family. A stream of tenants came and went after brief occupancies for the next hundred years. In the 1900's Wrens House was occupied by Baroness Vaux who used it as a summer residence. This poor lady could keep no staff, all left after a few days complaining that in parts of the house the atmosphere was unbearable. There is no record as to when the Baroness left, but the old house stayed empty for a number of years.

In the 1930's Wrens House was bought by two sisters with the unusual name of Outlaw. They turned it firstly into a tea shop and then an hotel.

The White Hart, Winkfield

Winkfield is the second largest parish in England. It seems to have an unexpected pub around every bend. The majority are ancient and interesting.

Arguably the most attractive of these is the White Hart. It has the perfect setting, opposite the church of St Mary, a building that is believed to date from the 13th century.

The White Hart is a little younger. Once again white and timbered, it comes on one of the many bends. A booklet provided by the hostelry states that the inn was a messuage (dwelling house with outbuildings and land) sold in 1593. It then became known as 'The Old Court House' and finally the White Hart.

Sir Christopher Wrens House Hotel, Windsor   Picture by Brenda Allaway

The White Hart, Winkfield   Picture by Peter Bourne

Ye Olde Hatchett, Winkfield

Strangely enough the name of this hostelry is almost unique. One would have thought it would have been prolific, considering the amount of forestry that once existed in this part of the country.

Ye Olde Hatchett was around in the 16th century when Winkfield, along with its neighbours Binfield and Warfield constituted the centre of the mighty Windsor Forest.

Along with a goodly number of other hostelries in the area, the Hatchett began life as a crofters cottage. As was the habit in those days, various crofters, foresters and woodmen brewed their own ale. It was mainly for the consumption of their family and that of their nearer neighbours. Thence saving the necessity of a trip into town.

Over the years a few of the more popular metamorphosed into beer houses and finally into pubs. The others sank into obscurity. The Hatchett was one of the survivors.

It is now a popular house for both locals and visitors. Internally and externally it has retained it ambience of pleasant antiquity. The Hatchett houses an old brass beer engine and its courtyard was once the venue for bare knuckle fighting bouts.

The Crooked Billet, Wokingham

Crooked Billets are some of the oldest hostelries in the country. The name is derived from a piece of firewood. The billet was a simple piece of wood with a right angle in it to name it easy to hang. It was the earliest ever form of advertising, the wood denoting that this was a place of lodging and sustenance long before the painted boards came into their own.

The sign is therefore not at all unusual. I can bring to mind at least half a dozen within a 25 mile radius of Wokingham. If the sign is not unusual, then the Crooked Billet at Wokingham certainly is for several reasons. It is at least a couple of miles from the town centre in an area known as Gardeners Green, which in turn is part of the tiny hamlet of St Sebastians.

There were once five pubs in this vicinity, three of which have subsequently disappeared. In the 1800's it was a wild and woolly territory populated by the hardy and tribalistic 'Broomdashers'.

These people, as their name suggests, made bessel brooms that were picked up by cart and delivered to Reading retailers. They were a remote and taciturn crowd living in abject poverty. Their homes were usually bivouacs, made from pulling down and tying young birch trees. Branches, ferns and moss were then added for weather proofing. At one time the broken glass ornaments with which they bedecked their homes were thought to be part of a pagan religion. A suspicious populace did not realise that these baubles were representative of poverty, not of a religious sect.

But to return to the Crooked Billet which was the favourite haunt of the 'Broomdashers' for many years. The inn was originally made of tongue and groove boards. The weather boarded facade remains today, its brilliant white frontage catching the eye as one rounds the bend from either direction.

What is not generally known is that in the late 19th century, the wooden structure was placed on rollers and transported from one side of the road to the other. The reason for such an expensive move is obscure, several reasons being put forward. I find one no more plausible than another. It is true that the Crooked Billet once brewed its own beer and it is suggested that had it remained in its original position it would have been hazardous to traffic. No doubt it would be today, but in the 1890's I would hardly think so.

My personal opinion is that it was a matter of finance. As previously stated, there are two bends nearby and in its original position it could not be seen from either. In its present position it can clearly be seen from both.

This was a locals pub for generations and still is to a degree, but its reputation for fine meals has attracted patrons from further afield. Of the many traditions associated with its antiquity, an ancient custom was revived for several years in the 1960's. The Crooked Mile was a race run by regulars once a year. It was a hazardous course, commencing down a very crooked lane next to the pub and across a ford in a stream, returning to the 'Billet' via another tortuous route. The winner receiving free beer for the day. Unfortunately the customs revival was very brief.

I am determined that the reader should not escape the Crooked Billet without hearing of the exploits of a previous landlord. A chapter of accidents of which I was blissfully unaware until I was researching the history of the area for my book 'The Crowthorne Chronicles' published in 1992. The following facts were gleaned from the columns of local newspapers.

Amongst other less notable achievements, in January 1865 at Wokingham Petty Sessions, William Goddard, Thomas Edwards and James Brown were charged with assaulting George Ewins, the landlord of the Crooked Billet. The charges were dropped owing to the complainant, Mr Ewins, being intoxicated in court and being mostly incoherent.

Later in January, George Ewins, along with George Miles the landlord of the Spotted Cow and George Bowens were charged with riotous behaviour and fined 5/- each. George Miles was also charged with opening a beer house before noon on a Sunday and fined 20/-.

In September 1865, George Ewins and landlord of the Crooked Billet, attempted suicide by throwing himself down his well. The well being nearly dry caused the attempt to be unsuccessful. Ewins was found over to keep the peace.

The Billet does not hit the headlines again until 1869 when Richard Shepherd the landlord was convicted of selling beer between three and five on Sunday 13 October and was fined 13/-. It seems that Mr Shepherd had inherited his predecessors flagrant disregard of the licensing authorities.

Ye Olde Hatchett, Winkfield   Picture by Brenda Allaway

Crooked Billet, Wokingham   Picture by Brenda Allaway

The Queens Head, Wokingham

This almost certainly Elizabethan inn stands on the terrace. The raised roadway at the start of the Reading Road at Wokingham in an area known as Shute End.

When one does a book on ancient inns. One is forever being tempted to overdo such adjectives as tasteful, charming, captivating, enchanting - one could go on forever.

A drawback to many old inns is that whilst accepting the suitability of the words mentioned above they are also often quite small and claustrophobic. Breweries find it impossible to expand because of the geographical location and preservation orders which restrict the amount of adaptation they can make to the exterior. A system which has both it assets and faults.

The Queens Head is the epitome of the ancient town inn. White walled, timbered, low beamed, leaded lights, etc., etc. The bars are small and three men stood together forms a crowd. The atmosphere is here, but one gets the yearning to make for the door every few minutes for fresh air. One gets the impression of a diver discovering an Alladins cave, but being forced to the surface at regular intervals.

The bar is once again tasteful, the panelled walls are adorned with cartoons of old cricket rules. There is probably a dozen stories to be related, all of which have disappeared from memory over the years.

The Olde Rose Inn, Wokingham

The Rose is a genuine Elizabethan inn. The counterfeit facade has tried to emulate as closely as possible the original design. In this case the alternations to the exterior were through necessity rather than choice as three mysterious fires in the last 25 years destroyed much of the pristine design.

In some places, the fires have most unfairly been blamed on The Rose's resident ghost. The spirit is one of a serving maid who was impregnated by the 19th century equivalent of a travelling salesman. Predictably he did not stand by her and the unfortunate maiden decided to end it all by hanging herself from a nearby tree.

This shade has manifested itself on several occasions in living memory. Each time in the dining room. I have a friend who swears that he was a lamp move of its own volition across the table, only coming to a halt when it reached the end of its electrical cable. There were at least three other diners present.

Why this unfortunate shade is blamed for the fires I have really no idea. If I may quote from my book 'Reputedly Haunted Inns of the Chilterns and Thames Valley', "If logic exists in the spirit world, why should this poor unhappy spectre be quite content to harmlessly float through kitchen and restaurant for some 150 years, and then become a raging pyromaniac for a brief 15 years in the 1960's and 1970's - most unlikely."

A well authenticated and too often related tale of The Rose is that Gay, Swift, Pope and Arbruthnot whiled away an hour or two by composing verses to Molly Mogg, an attractive barmaid. John Arbruthnot was a Scottish physician and writer who was a fellow of the University College at Oxford (not a lot of people know that).

However I deviate, Molly Mogg is supposed to have become Molly Miller and it is her buxom form that greets visitors to Wokingham as they dismount from a train. I personally believe there is no relationship whatsoever. Wokingham was inundated with inns in the early 18th century. The name Molly was as common then as say Rebecca or Emma are today, or as Jackie was in my day. I do not believe that it is beyond the laws of possibility that Wokingham hostelries had a couple of attractive Molly's.

Generally, the sign of The Rose commemorates the confrontation of the houses of York and Lancashire. Some, as this one does, were put there to suggest that the inn was wholesome and attractive. Hence the lovely english rose. Incidentally, the Duke of Wellington was a regular patron of The Rose. He used it as a stop off place on his way to his estate at Stratfield Saye.

The Queens Head   Picture by Brenda Allaway

The Olde Rose Inn, Wokingham   Picture by Peter Bourne

The Red Lion, Wokingham

In 1661, George Staverton, a wealthy if henpecked businessman of Wokingham, bequeathed the sum of £6 a year to provide the town with a bull. The animal was to be used for bull baiting each St thomas' eve (21 December). The princely sum enabled this spectacle to be indulged in by the townsfolk form some 162 years until its final abolition.

Wokingham was notorious for bull baiting, cock fighting and bare knuckle boxing. When bull bating was in session every down and out and drifter for miles around descended to the town. Many extra constables were drafted in to maintain law and order. Total chaos would ensue when young bulls were loosed in the streets. Several people lost their lives as they were tramples underfoot. In 1794 Elizabeth North died after being terribly bruised. Martha May met the same fate after being trampled by the Wokingham Fighters, a group of ferocious felons. Other reports tell of a man who was not expected to live when found trampled in Cockpit Path. It was rumoured, but never proven that incompatible spouses found it a felicitous opportunity to rid themselves of their partners in marriage.

Be that as it may, the Red Lion yard was where many of the bulls were stabled. The yard also housed the strutting cocks prior to their antagonistic and barbaric battles to the death at the cockpit. The alley way adjacent to the Red Lion is still named Cockpit Path. The noise in the inns yard must have been more that a little disconcerting for the neighbours. On second thoughts, most of the Red Lions neighbours were pubs with similar inclinations, there were 15 just around the old town hall.

The Red Lion is adjoined upstairs with another gabled property that once was the Kings Head. A coach way leads between the two inns. The Red Lion has been altered much inside, albeit tastefully and in keeping with its revered age. Wooden panelling and beams are prevalent. An ancient cash till is in the front bar.

Incidentally, the Red Lion, like many other pubs, has a nickname. Several that spring to mind are Cutthroat Kates, so called because of an attempt on the landlady's life with a razor. The Black Swan becomes the Mucky Duck. A pub at Sandhurst became the Shit and Shovel because of its close proximity to a sewerage farm. In Crowthorne another pub whose proprietor George married a rather tenacious woman, became known as the George and Dragon.

The Red Lion, back in the days when I worked opposite in W.H. Smiths, has a very colourful couple of hosts. The lady was of french extract, middle aged but exceedingly slim and fit. She lived on Guiness and could kick her legs to the ceiling. The husband was somewhat older, more sedate and sported a small goatee beard. It did not take much imagination from the locals to turn the Red Lion to the Frog and Goat.

In general, Red Lion's throughout the country were named in appreciation of John of Gaunt, one of the country's most respected heroes who was popularised by Shakespeare in King Richard II.

The Ship, Wokingham

The building of the ship is over 400 years old. As a pub however, it has been in existence for about half that time. Although many extensions have been built in what can best be described as a somewhat haphazard manner, much of the original building still exists.

During one of the renovations, the main bar was altered and a large oven was discovered. The existence of this gave rise to the supposition that the building was once a bakery. This may well have been the case. At one time nearly every small business in the town had a subsidiary concern, and in most cases this had something to do with the licensing trade. Bars were later attached to nearly every small business and subsequently a swinging sign appeared. For example, in an early trade directory of Wokingham,k such entries appear as James Prior of the Robin Hood (also a bricklayer) and James Hope of the Pin and Bowl (also a shoemaker). However, ironically enough William Wickens of The Ship is not listed as a baker, but as a carrier.

The Ship was no doubt a coach house at one stage, as were most of the Wokingham inns. A vast stable, now demolished, endorsed this fact and it is pretty well established that the building once included the inevitable coffee shop.

A reported from a local paper in the late 1970's included an interview with the landlord who insisted that the place was haunted. Weird noises were heard emulating from an alcove in a small room situated above the patio doors. The landlord stated that he had inspected the room, and no hot water pipes, often blamed for such occurrences, went anywhere near the suspect area.

Some information I have recently gleaned is that there was more poltergeist activity as late as 1989. A relief manager heard noises coming from the cellar, stalls were dragged across the room and pots and pans rattled of their own volition. The managers dog found the cellar most disconcerting indeed.

Be that as it may, it must obviously be put down to speculation. The Ship today has an intriguing rather than foreboding atmosphere. Rooms seem to traverse in every direction. The decor is pleasant and pictures of ancient mariners are abundant. Collections of unbelievably intricate seaman's knots are displayed in glass cases. A ships figurehead of a female form, tastelessly displaying and exposed breast, is tucked away in the lounge bar. There is a pleasing and agreeable atmosphere at The Ship, almost unique in this day and age.

Red Lion, Wokingham					Picture by Peter Bourne

The Ship, Wokingham					Picture by Peter Bourne

The Three Frogs

A most deceiving little pub on the London Road near the outskirts of the town. It is deceptive because apparently its appearance belies its great age. There must have been several substantial alterations.

The Three Frogs is pleasantly panelled inside and one risks repeating the word cosy. An enterprising landlord has adorned parts of the room with extremely vivid photographs of lime green frogs. One monster stared at you from behind the bar in the lounge.

How the Three Frogs got is name is always worth causing a heated discussion in Wokingham. There is so very little evidence and so much speculative conjecture. It is almost certainly the only inn of this name in the country. Indisputably we have Frog Hall and Frog Hall Drive just across the busy London Road, but this is a chicken and egg situation, the inn probably outdates the hall by several centuries.

Here's one explanation that is as acceptable as any other. In the 15th century the inn was known as the 'Sheaths of Barley'. It showed three sheaths of barley on the sign. The landlord, a Belgian entrepreneur pre-empted the common market by serving his customers frogs-legs. God alone knows where he got them from. I am told the British variety are inedible and if he received them by coach from the continent they would have been a little overripe on arrival. Be that as it may the innkeeper thought it advantageous to advertise these delicacies on his signboard. He also thought it prudent to get a local painter to daub over his original sign of three barley sheaths with three frogs.

That's the story anyway and I'll stick by it until someone comes up with a better one.

Angel, Woolhampton

This is a magnificent ivy clad old coaching inn, fronting on to the A4. It is justly famous for its home cooked food, its skittle alley and a wide choice of traditional ales.

It has a restaurant separate from the bar room. The bar room is interesting in the extreme, more modern amusements compliment rather than contradict the ancient local scenes that adorn the wall. Several interesting autographs are depicted above the bar, King William I rubs shoulders with Lord John Russel, one time prime minister of England. For no apparent reason there is also a 1879 soup kitchen ticket on display. One wonders what type of culinary adventure one would have on presentation of the above, its price, 1 penny.

The Angel was one of the enterprising inns that, in the 18th century, supplied it own tokens for the purchase of alcohol on the premises.

The Three Frogs, Wokingham   Picture by Peter Bourne

The Angel, Woolhampton   Picture by Brenda Allaway

The Rising Sun, Woolhampton

The sign of the Rising Sun is one of Britains most popular boards. It is generally thought to honour Edward III from who's coat of arms it is taken. There is also a theory, although less likely, that it commemorates Richard III. It later became a sign of the distillers.

The Rising Sun at Woolhampton is an old coaching inn directly beside the old Bath Road (A4). It has been much altered over the years, but remains in the most part anyway, representative of its original function.

The inn has a couple of stories to tell, both to do with highwaymen which is typical enough of its story. One tells of Captain Hawkes, a much admired footpad and a master of disguise. Hawkes was dressed as a quaker at the Plough Inn at Salt Hill near Slough. An affluent stranger came in and looked searchingly around the room, seeing only a poor quaker he felt at ease enough to place his pistols and valuables on the inns table. He blustered a warning to the quaker that the should not travel the roads unarmed with such as Captain Hawkes was in the vicinity. After a further word of conversation he finished his vitals and left.

On the western side of Reading the traveller was robbed by a masked highwayman. He attempted to shoot his assailant but his pistols failed to fire, leaving him at the mercy of the robber. He did however, recognise his assailant as being the quaker of his earlier acquaintance.

After relieving the gentleman of his valuables, Hawkes warned him against showing his valuables and leaving his firearms where they could be interfered with. Unfortunately for Hawkes, it was his last hold-up. That night he repaired to the Rising Sun at Woolhampton where he sat enjoying his supper. Feeling at ease with the world after a good days takings, Hawkes engaged in conversation with a couple of country yokels that were playing card at a nearby table.

A quarrel developed between the two card payers as one accused the other of cheating. The row developed violently to the extent that one of the protagonists drew a knife from his belt. Hoping to pacify the situation, Hawkes intervened only to find he was instantly grabbed by the yokels, both being Bow Street Runners in disguise, the tell-tale red tunics now being displayed from under their country smocks.

Hawkes was escorted to Newgate and from thence to Tyburn where he followed countless others of his profession.

The second story is of the same ilk, if somewhat shorter to relate. The Reading Mercury of May 1983, states that two brothers named Hazell of Midgham were returning home in a one horse chaise when near the Rising Sun inn at Woolhampton they were attacked by four villains. The gentlemen were badly beaten and deprived of their valuables. The crawled to the Rising Sun where a posse was organised, probably to no avail.

There was however, a reward of £10 offered for information leading to an arrest. The outcome of this enticement is unknown.

The Royal Oak, Yattendon

A famous pub that has been well acclaimed in local history over the years. It has won many prizes and still proudly maintains its status.

It was reputedly haunted years ago. Just a few creaks and rumbles as far as my research can make out.

Haunted or not there is a tragedy in the old pubs history. In 1956 Mrs Faithful fell to her death. The floor of the inn opened up and the poor woman fell 134 feet down a disused well shaft.

It has been estimated that there are some 140 disused wells in the area. It should deem this unlikely as this would average about two wells to each dwelling. Be that as it may, there is a local legend that one such well secretes a fortune. A horde of gold left by a fleeing family during the civil war. Many searches have been made, but nothing as yet has surfaced.

The Rising Sun, Woolhampton   Picture by Brenda Allaway

The Royal Oak, Yattendon   Picture by Brenda Allaway